Monophonic Tropes
and Conductus of W1

Recent Researches in Music

A-R Editions publishes seven series of critical editions, spanning the history of Western music, American music, and oral traditions.

Recent Researches in the Music of the Middle Ages and Early Renaissance
    Charles M. Atkinson, general editor

Recent Researches in the Music of the Renaissance
    James Haar, general editor

Recent Researches in the Music of the Baroque Era
    Christoph Wolff, general editor

Recent Researches in the Music of the Classical Era
    Neal Zaslaw, general editor

Recent Researches in the Music of the Nineteenth and Early Twentieth Centuries
    Rufus Hallmark, general editor

Recent Researches in American Music
    John M. Graziano, general editor

Recent Researches in the Oral Traditions of Music
    Philip V. Bohlman, general editor

Each edition in *Recent Researches* is devoted to works by a single composer or to a single genre. The content is chosen for its high quality and historical importance and is edited according to the scholarly standards that govern the making of all reliable editions.

For information on establishing a standing order to any of our series, or for editorial guidelines on submitting proposals, please contact:

A-R Editions, Inc.
Middleton, Wisconsin

800 736-0070 (North American book orders)
608 836-9000 (phone)
608 831-8200 (fax)
http://www.areditions.com

RECENT RESEARCHES IN THE MUSIC OF THE MIDDLE AGES AND EARLY RENAISSANCE, 38

Monophonic Tropes and Conductus of W1

The Tenth Fascicle

Edited by Jann Cosart

A-R Editions, Inc.
Middleton, Wisconsin

In memoriam Thomas Binkley

The facsimile reproduces Herzog August Bibliothek Wolfenbüttel, Cod. Guelf. 628 Helmst., Fascicle X. It is printed with the permission of the Herzog August Bibliothek, Wolfenbüttel.

A-R Editions, Inc., Middleton, Wisconsin
© 2007 by A-R Editions, Inc.

All rights reserved. No part of this book may be reproduced or transmitted in any form by any electronic or mechanical means (including photocopying, recording, or information storage and retrieval) without permission in writing from the publisher.

The purchase of this edition does not convey the right to perform it in public, nor to make a recording of it for any purpose. Such permission must be obtained in advance from the publisher.

A-R Editions is pleased to support scholars and performers in their use of *Recent Researches* material for study or performance. Subscribers to any of the *Recent Researches* series, as well as patrons of subscribing institutions, are invited to apply for information about our "Copyright Sharing Policy."

Printed in the United States of America

ISBN-13: 978-0-89579-622-6
ISBN-10: 0-89579-622-8
ISSN: 0362-3572

♾ The paper used in this publication meets the minimum requirements of the American National Standard for Information Sciences—Permanence of Paper for Printed Library Materials, ANSI Z39.48-1992.

Contents

Sigla   vii

Acknowledgments   viii

Introduction   ix

  The Manuscript   ix
  Conductus   x
  Tropes   xi
  Rhythm   xv
  Notes on Performance   xviii
  Notes   xx

Texts and Translations   xxiv

Facsimile   xxxiii

Monophonic Tropes and Conductus of W1

Conductus

  1. Quomodo cantabimus   3
  2. Ve mundo a scandalis   4
  3. In Rama sonat gemitus   5

Sanctus Tropes

  4. Sanctus Christe yerarchia   6
  5. Sanctus Rex qui cuncta regis   10
  6. Sanctus Omnia qui libras   12
  7. Sanctus Cunctorum dominans   14
  8. Sanctus Condita de nichilo   16
  9. Sanctus Sanctus ab eterno   18

Agnus Tropes

  10. Agnus Archetipi mundi   20
  11. Agnus Pectoris alta   22
  12. Agnus Qui de virgineo   24
  13. Agnus Lux lucis   25
  14. Agnus Humano generi   27
  15. Agnus Vulnere quorum   28

Critical Report   31

  Editorial Methods   31
  Critical Notes   32

Appendix
  Sanctus: PBN 1112   37
  Sanctus: Reconstructed from W1   37
  Agnus dei: PBN 1112   38
  Critical Notes   38

Sigla

Assisi 695	Assisi, Biblioteca comunale, 695.
Bar 1408/9	Barcelona, Biblioteca central, frag. 1408/IX.
Berlin 40171	Berlin, Staatsbibliothek, Mus. 40171.
Da	Darmstadt, Hessische Landes- und Hochschulbibliothek, 3471.
DeZayas	DeZayas Troper (private collection).
Du 6	Durham, University Library, Cosin V.II.6.
F	Florence, Biblioteca Medicea-Laurenziana, pluteus 29.1.
Fauv	Paris, Bibliothèque nationale, fonds fr. 146.
Hu	Burgos, Monasterio de Las Huelgas.
Iv 60	Ivrea, Biblioteca capitolare, LX.
La 263	Laon, Bibliothèque municipale, 263.
Li 2(17)	Limoges, Bibliothèque municipale, 2(17).
Lo 2B.IV	London, British Library, Royal 2 B.IV.
Lo 12194	London, British Library, Add. 12,194.
Lo 13	London, British Library, Royal 8 C.XIII.
Ma 288	Madrid, Biblioteca nacional, 288.
Ma 289	Madrid, Biblioteca nacional, 289.
Ma 19421	Madrid, Biblioteca nacional, 19421.
OxB 775	Oxford, Bodleian Library, 775.
OxB b5	Oxford, Bodleian Library, lat. lit. b.5.
PBA 135	Paris, Bibliothèque de l'Arsenal, 135.
PBN 1112	Paris, Bibliothèque nationale, fonds lat. 1112.
PBN 1235	Paris, Bibliothèque nationale, n.a. lat. 1235.
PBN 2298	Paris, Bibliothèque nationale, fonds lat. 2298.
PBN 3126	Paris, Bibliothèque nationale, n.a. lat. 3126.
PBN 7185	Paris, Bibliothèque nationale, fonds lat. 7185.
PBN 9449	Paris, Bibliothèque nationale, fonds lat. 9449.
PBN 10508	Paris, Bibliothèque nationale, fonds lat. 10508.
PBN 10511	Paris, Bibliothèque nationale, fonds lat. 10511.
Sab	Rome, Santa Sabina, XIV L. 3
SG 378	St. Gall, Stiftsbibliothek, Hs. 378.
SG 382	St. Gall, Stiftsbibliothek, Hs. 382.
SG 383	St. Gall, Stiftsbibliothek, Hs. 383.
SG 546	St. Gall, Stiftsbibliothek, Hs. 546.
SL HB I.95	Stuttgart, Landesbibliothek, HB.I.95.
St-M C	Paris, Bibliothèque nationale, fonds lat. 3719.
Tours	Tours, Bibliothèque municipale, 927.
W1	Wolfenbüttel, Herzog August Bibliothek, Cod. Guelf. 628 Helmst.
W2	Wolfenbüttel, Herzog August Bibliothek, Cod. Guelf. 1099 Helmst.
Wor 160	Worcester, Cathedral Chapter Library, F.160.

Acknowledgments

There are many people and institutions who contributed to this edition; here I can name but a few. The late Thomas Binkley supplied the idea for this project many years ago, and his guiding spirit continues to provide inspiration. In my work with the Latin texts, I was very fortunate to have the assistance of Benito Rivera, of Indiana University, and Byron Stayskal. Byron was especially generous with his time and expertise, going over my translations with a keen eye and offering a multitude of helpful suggestions. In fact, many of the phrases incorporate Byron's skillful translations.

I am also grateful for the help of Baylor University, which supported this study in part with a research leave and funds from the Baylor University Research Committee, enabling me to travel to Wolfenbüttel to consult the original source. In Wolfenbüttel, the entire staff of the Herzog August Bibliothek was gracious and helpful to my research. I especially want to thank Alexandra Ilginus, Marina Arnold, and Restorer Heinrich Grau for their knowledgeable assistance at the library, their accommodating long-distance correspondence, and their kind permission to publish the present edition and the facsimiles. I also thank the staff of A-R Editions, Inc., for the editing and preparation of this volume for publication.

Finally, I am most indebted to my husband Timothy Johnson, and my daughter Maya, who both endured many long hours, late nights, and frozen pizzas on my behalf.

Introduction

Manuscript W1 is one of the most highly regarded collections of early polyphony. It holds a pivotal and important place in history as one of the three principal surviving medieval manuscripts of the *Magnus Liber*, the "great book" of twelfth-century polyphony associated with the cathedral of Notre Dame in Paris,[1] and its history has been investigated by many scholars. The inscription on folio 64, "liber monasterij S. andree apostoli in scocia," suggests a connection with St. Andews in Scotland, and although there are few extant medieval liturgical manuscripts with music from St. Andrews to compare with W1, scholars have convincingly tied the codex both to St. Andrews[2] and to Notre Dame Cathedral in Paris.[3] While it was first thought that the manuscript may date from the fourteenth century, more recent evidence shows that it was likely compiled in the thirteenth century.[4] Future studies may generate more definitive conclusions about the date and provenance of W1,[5] but the current cumulative evidence points toward a relationship between Paris and St. Andrews, and a dating within the early and the early-mid thirteenth century.

Despite the many studies of W1, few have mentioned the single-line, monophonic liturgical chants tucked away near the end of the manuscript in the tenth fascicle. This section contains fifteen pieces that fall into two stylistically contrasting genres: conductus and tropes. Over half of the texts and all but two of the melodies are unica (see "Critical Notes" in the critical report for a complete list of concordances), and the tropes are strikingly melismatic in comparison with other contemporary tropes (see "Tropes: Overview of the Trope Concordances" below). Given the probable connection with St. Andrews, this unusual collection may contain clues to lost Scottish or Celtic Christian worship. Little music of this type has been preserved in Ireland itself: the few manuscripts of medieval Celtic rites contain either no musical notation, or very sketchy information at best. Therefore, the chants of W1 are of considerable importance to a wide range of scholars. This edition is the first complete publication of the monophonic repertoire of W1.

The Manuscript

W1 is located in the Herzog August Bibliothek in Wolfenbüttel, Germany, cataloged as "Codex Guelf. 628 Helmstadiensis."[6] The manuscript measures ca. 21 x 15 cm and consists of 197 leaves of three grades of parchment, marked with two sets of foliations on recto pages.[7] The first foliation is inked in the center of the upper recto sides in a late medieval hand using roman numerals until folio xxix, continuing with arabic numerals from 30; the second is a late-nineteenth-century arabic numbering penciled in the upper right corner. The first numbering is more complete, as it demonstrates where pages are now missing, and thus it will be used throughout this study.

W1 contains eleven fascicles compiled from twenty- seven gatherings, each fascicle loosely grouping similar compositions. Fascicle I contains four-voice organa, and Fascicle II is dedicated to primarily three-voice organa. Two-voice compositions are contained in the next four groupings: organa for the office (Fascicle III), fifty-nine organa for the mass (Fascicle IV), and clausulae (Fascicles V and VI). Fascicle VII, like Fascicle II, contains three-voice organa, and the eighth fascicle also has three-part compositions: organa, but also conductus and tropes. The ninth and eleventh fascicles hold primarily two-voice conductus and two-voice compositions for Marian masses.

The tenth fascicle is the only grouping that contains monophonic music. This fascicle originally consisted of two quaternia—gatherings 23 and 24—the first of which is missing. Gathering 24, folios 185–92, begins in the middle of a conductus and continues with two more conductus and twelve tropes for two Ordinary chants: six on the Sanctus and six on the Agnus Dei (see table 1).[8] The two conductus plus the fragmented third are most likely the end of an entire section of

ix

TABLE 1
Diagram of W1 Fascicle X

Folios: Staves*		
Start	End	Item
177	184	[missing gathering]
185r:1	185r:4	Quomodo cantabimus (last section)
185r:5	185v:4	Ve mundo a scandalis
185v:5	185v:8	In Rama sonat gemitus
185v:9	186v:5	Sanctus Christe yerarchia
186v:6	187r:5	Sanctus Rex qui cuncta regis
187r:6	187v:7	Sanctus Omnia qui libras
187v:8	188r:8	Sanctus Cunctorum dominans
188r:9	188v:9	Sanctus Condita de nichilo
188v:10	189r:6	Sanctus Sanctus ab eterno
189r:7	189v:7	Agnus Archetipi mundi
189v:8	190r:7	Agnus Pectoris alta
190r:8	190v:5	Agnus Qui de virgineo
190v:6	191r:1	Agnus Lux lucis
191r:2	191r:9	Agnus Humano generi
191r:10	191v:8	Agnus Vulnere quorum
191v:9	191v:9	colophon
191v:10	192v	[blank staves]

*Numbers following colons refer to particular staves on the cited folios.

monophonic conductus we now lack because of the missing gathering.

Fascicle X has an individual ruling: each folio consists of ten five-line staves drawn in red ink. These staves are like those drawn for the upper polyphonic voices in other W1 fascicles but contrast with the four-line staves used for the tenor lines. Perhaps Fascicle X's wide melodic range and florid style encouraged the scribe to choose the staff of the new polyphonic voices instead of the standard four-line notation of monophonic chant. After the last trope, a later colophon at the bottom of folio 191v indicates the end of the scribe's work (see facsimile of fol. 191v).[9] The last folio in the gathering (192) is filled with blank five-line staves on both sides, the words "equore" and "omnibus" in the upper right recto margin.[10]

The main body of the manuscript contains the work of two or three scribes whose hands are very similar. Slight variations in the dimensions of the ruling suggest that one scribe wrote at least the opening five fascicles, as well as Fascicles VIII–X.[11] It is clear that Fascicle X is part of the original manuscript, because of the hand and ruling, but also because of the wear patterns of the manuscript. Although the first gathering of the tenth fascicle is missing, the leaf immediately preceding Fascicle X (fol. 176) is not worn down, as it would be had it been the last page of an independent grouping at one time. Similarly, the first extant folio of Fascicle X (fol. 185), which begins the second gathering, does not show signs of wear. On the other hand, the last folio of this second gathering (fol. 192) clearly demonstrates the end of a compilation. The recto side is not numbered in the older foliation hand and the top staff is very faint, and on the verso side all of the blank staves are almost completely worn off. Thus, the tenth fascicle, although it contains an idiosyncratic repertoire, is part of the main body of the manuscript.

The musical notation throughout W1 is square notation with black ink. The C clef is the only pitch indication used in the tenth fascicle. It is drawn consistently at the beginning of each staff,[12] most often on the third line, but sometimes on the fourth line, and twice on the second line. Clef changes serve to avoid ledger lines and are almost always at the beginning of a line. There are a small number of *fa* (♭) signs to indicate lowered notes within the body of the compositions, and also, although it is uncommon for the time period, two examples of *mi* (♮) signs that clarify cancellation of the flat.[13] For the most part, there is little question about pitches.

The note shapes are puncta (both square and rhomboid), virga, and ligatures that consist largely of square-shaped notes but also, less often, liquescent forms. In addition, there are a number of descending plicae.[14] The music notation of the tenth fascicle looks similar to that in other parts of W1: the note shapes conform essentially to the conventions established throughout—with the exception of the large number of melismatic, diamond-shaped rhombi, which the thirteenth-century writer Anonymous IV calls currentes.[15]

Conductus

The first two conductus of Fascicle X have concordances in several other manuscripts, which fortunately allows reconstruction of the fragmentary first piece. W1's tenth fascicle begins on the fifth line of *Quomodo cantabimus* (no. 1), but the entire composition is notated in manuscript F (fol. 425v), where two additional text verses are also provided. The satirical poem by Philip the Chancellor criticizes current ways and customs of the clergy.[16] Lines 7–8 include a direct reference to the crucifixion scene in John 19:23–24, where the soldiers cast lots for Jesus's one-piece tunic instead of tearing it. The poetic scenario, in which Jesus displays torn clothing, stands in biting contrast with the biblical passage, perhaps to imply that the persons under critique are somehow responsible for Jesus's ragged appearance. One long poetic stanza can be grouped in four-line units of alternating rhyme, extended by an inserted couplet preceding the second four-line unit *(abab ccc'dc'd efef)*. The incisive text was apparently still appropriate a century later, when it was reworked into motet form in the *Roman de Fauvel*, set to different music with an interesting twist: the texts of the first two stanzas are sung simultaneously as motetus and triplum over an untexted, unidentified tenor.[17]

Ve mundo a scandalis (no. 2), a planctus, adds the element of lamentation. The text bemoans the people enslaved by Rome, starved by tax collectors, while at the same time warning those in power that God's day of judgment will come. W1 lays out this powerful message in three strophes. Concordant manuscripts differ in the number of strophes they present for this piece,[18] but all divide the strophes into unequal lengths: the outer verses are similar, consisting of six lines each and a matching rhyme pattern, while the inside verse is composed of eight lines and a simple alternating rhyme scheme *(aabccb bdbdbdbd eefggf)*. Although combined in various ways, all of the lines are octosyllabic. The poetry is attributed to Philip the Chancellor in the concordant manuscript Da, but this authorship is now thought to be doubtful.[19]

Both *Quomodo cantabimus* and *Ve mundo a scandalis* are through-composed. *Quomodo cantabimus* is written especially freely, not relying on repeating music or cadential patterns. Its range (d–g')[20] fills the combined ambitus of Mixolydian and Hypomixolydian melodic modes, although the tessitura falls mainly within the Hypomixolydian octave d–d'. The text setting is predominantly syllabic and neumatic; the exceptions are the expressive, long melismas at the beginnings of sections, and the extended melisma before the final cadence. *Ve mundo a scandalis* has the same range as *Quomodo cantabimus,* but the G *finalis* and B♭ key signature define the mode as transposed Dorian. The setting weaves together and links its three text verses, blurring the natural text divisions. Each verse begins (and sometimes ends) with a melisma, punctuating an otherwise syllabic or neumatic setting.[21] W1's melodies for *Quomodo cantabimus* and *Ve mundo a scandalis* are very similar to those notated in concordant manuscript F, although W1's melismas are more extensive. It is interesting to note the similar layout of the two manuscripts: in both, the last four lines of *Quomodo cantabimus* are sectioned off by a large initial letter *O* and this piece is immediately followed by the three-verse *Ve mundo a scandalis*.

In Rama sonat gemitus (no. 3), an unicum, is rich with historical and biblical reference. Although not named explicitly, the poetry alludes to Thomas Becket, archbishop of Canterbury, and his exile from England to France because of disagreements with Henry II. The poignant lament associates Becket's exile with the Holy Family's flight into Egypt (see Matthew 2:18 in the Revised Standard Version: "A voice was heard in Ramah, wailing and loud lamentation, Rachel weeping for her children") and also with Rachel's first-born, Joseph, who was sold into slavery in Egypt (Genesis 37). A third reference is provided by means of a visual allusion to the archbishop: *In Rama sonat gemitus* begins with an elaborate initial *I* (fol. 185v), which extends into the left margin in the shape of a bishop's staff.[22] These references outline a framework for dating the piece; namely during the six years of Becket's exile, between 1164 and 1170.

The poetry is laid out in eight lines, each with eight syllables. The lines have a consistent stress on the antepenultimate syllable and alternate methodically with a two-part rhyme scheme *(ab ab ab ab)*. The musical setting reflects the regularity of the poetry, in contrast with the through-composed, free nature of the two preceding conductus. The first musical phrase returns for text line 3 and repeats with variation for line 6. The last two lines receive different music and function as a closing couplet. The piece is in the Dorian mode, with a standard range of the octave plus one note on either side: c–e'. Last notes of lines alternate between D and F, except the penultimate line, which stops on E, pulling the melody down to the final D. Cadence formulae can be analyzed similarly, with an alternation of two patterns until the closing couplet, which introduces a third and fourth. These characteristics all fit neatly together to create a transparent organization:

Line Number	1	2	3	4	5	6	7	8
Text Rhyme	a	b	a	b	a	b	a	b
Musical Form	A	B	A	B	C	A'	D	E
Last Note	F	D	F	D	F	F	E	D
Cadence Formula	α	β	α	β	α'	α	γ	δ

Text setting is syllabic or neumatic; the melismas and caudae of the previous two conductus are noticeably absent. The piece has more in common with some of the earlier Notre Dame conductus and Parisian sequences than with any of the surrounding material in W1.[23] In fact, *In Rama sonat gemitus* easily qualifies as the earliest composition in all of W1, both by its musical style and its specific text references.

Tropes

Study of the W1 tropes requires an investigation of the parent chants on which the tropes are based, as the chants are the foundation for the elaborated settings.

Equally beneficial is a comparison with the concordant tropes, which shed light on the parent melodies and the treatment of the inserted poetry. Each of these items is considered separately in preparation for a more detailed analytical discussion of the W1 tropes.

Parent Chants

W1 notates the newly added trope material in full, but its representation of the parent-chant framework is sketchy. Although the chants are not complete, there are extraordinarily explicit guides for realizing them; the fascicle consistently includes incipits for each section. This practice contrasts with the tropes in other fascicles of W1, for example, which only give a brief cue at the beginning of the piece.[24] The incipits indicate that all of the Sanctus and Agnus tropes in W1, Fascicle X, have the same respective parent chant. Reconstruction of the implied texts is not problematic, even in the sparsely cued fascicles of W1, since they were standardized among all regions by this period. It is necessary, however, to consult other sources in order to complete the omitted music.

Although there were standardized melodies for the chants of the Ordinary in the Middle Ages, these melodies did vary from region to region, and thus a search for the most precise match logically begins with manuscripts that share a regional proximity with W1. Among sources associated with the British isles, the thirteenth-century Lo 12194 transmits Sanctus and Agnus chant versions that come close to the St. Andrews tradition. The melodies are not exactly the same, however; W1 displays internal phrase variants from these Sarum melodies. Because the polyphonic music in W1 is clearly from the Paris Notre Dame tradition, the next obvious sources to consult are continental ones, and as one might expect, an examination of a thirteenth-century Parisian missal, PBN 1112, proves to be fruitful.[25] Near the end of the manuscript, there is a small kyriale that contains five Sanctus and six Agnus melodies, among which are very close matches to the W1 Sanctus and Agnus chants (see the appendix for transcriptions). I have inserted material from these chants, modified as described below, to complete the tropes in the edition.

The first Sanctus in PBN 1112 is troped (*Sanctus Perpetuo numine,* fol. 307v), but fortunately, the PBN music scribe took the unusual step of writing out the parent melody in full, including the last "Osanna." It appears to be the same parent melody that W1's scribe abbreviates in Fascicle X. This particular Sanctus is listed in Thannabauer's catalog as no. 49.[26] The melody is quite common and was popular from the eleventh through the eighteenth centuries.[27] The music of this Sanctus does not contain repeated sections, but it does have large portions of musical rhyme: the third

"Sanctus" starts like the first but has a slightly different ending, and the words "in excelsis" have the same melody as the combined second and third "Sanctus." The musical form of the PBN 1112 Sanctus is thus:

Sanctus. Sanctus. Sanctus.	ABA'
Dominus deus sabaoth.	C
Pleni sunt celi et terra gloria tua.	D
Osanna in excelsis.	EBA'
Benedictus qui venit in nomine domini.	F
Osanna in excelsis.	GBA'

A comparison of the PBN 1112 Sanctus with the incipits of the W1 tropes reveals two minor differences. First, the third "Sanctus" of the W1 tropes is consistently notated the same as the first, creating an ABA structure in contrast with the ABA' of PBN 1112. This small variant has led me to make a minor adjustment in the "Osanna in excelsis" fleshed out from PBN 1112: to be true to the musical poetics of the PBN 1112 version, both occurrences of "Osanna in excelsis" should rhyme musically with "Sanctus. Sanctus. Sanctus," but since W1 requires that the "Sanctus" line end with music A (not A'), I have replaced all A' sections from PBN 1112 with the unvaried music A. The second notable difference occurs on the word "sabaoth,"[28] where ligature patterns and pitches are slightly different in the two versions:

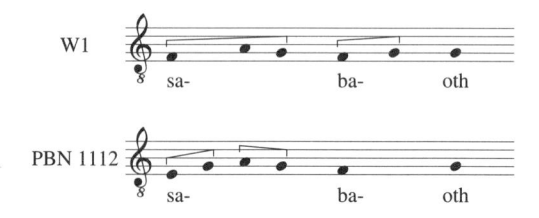

As with the earlier A/A' variation, I have made the assumption that this W1 melody was sung for all of the tropes; I thus used this material and not the PBN 1112 version in reconstructing the Sanctus melody. (My composite melody, constructed from both W1 and PBN 1112 phrases, is given in the appendix along with the unaltered PBN 1112 version.)

The Agnus chant that is traceable from the W1 Agnus tropes is very similar to the one cataloged by Schildbach as Agnus 136, a melody that was popular during the twelfth through sixteenth centuries.[29] The W1 version, however, is written in G, up a tone from the usual version in F.[30] This feature unites it with the first Agnus in PBN 1112, also written in G, and all of the W1 trope incipits compare favorably with the PBN 1112 version (*Agnus Archetipi mundi* adheres exactly, while the following five tropes transmit a consistent variant on the first and third "Agnus," a repercussion on the second note). The music is similar to the Sanctus melody in that it contains melodic rhyme, adhering to the text divisions, and unfolds in a rounded tripartite form (here written as ACA because of the similar B endings), as shown below:

Agnus dei qui tollis peccata mundi	A
miserere nobis.	B
Agnus dei qui tollis peccata mundi	C
miserere nobis.	B
Agnus dei qui tollis peccata mundi	A
dona nobis pacem.	B

Overview of the Trope Concordances

Five of the W1 trope texts survive in other manuscripts as well. Some of the concordances follow W1 in elaborating the same chant, while others use completely different material. A comparison between the *Sanctus Rex qui cuncta regis* versions in W1 and SG 378 is somewhat inconclusive because the St. Gall neumes in SG 378 lack precise pitch information. To add to this ambiguity, the first two "Sanctus" incipits are not notated; however, the melodic gestures on the third "Sanctus" are representative of W1's parent chant, Sanctus 49. The melody notated for the trope text, on the other hand, is very different from and much simpler than that of W1. For example, the melisma for the word "Rex" in W1 lasts almost an entire staff line, while the analogous gesture in SG 378 is only a few neumes.

Another St. Gall concordance, SG 383, appears to be the same *Sanctus Rex qui cuncta regis* as SG 378, but in a more definitive square notation with clearer references to the Sanctus 49 melody.[31] This manuscript also contains two other W1 tropes: a version of *Sanctus Omnia qui libras*, and a variation of *Agnus Archetipi mundi* in which the Sanctus, not the Agnus, serves as the parent chant.[32] Both of these settings elaborate Sanctus 49, but again with melodies that differ from W1's. The W1 and SG 383 versions of *Sanctus Omnia qui libras* begin similarly with G repeated, but they diverge immediately in the first melisma.[33] The two *Archetipi mundi* melodies are completely different except that they both contain lengthy melismas on similar syllables.

Among the W1 Agnus tropes, the *Agnus Lux lucis* has by far the largest number of concordant texts. The version in manuscript Assisi 695 has different chant (Schildbach Agnus 267) and trope melodies than W1 and is thus a completely different piece of music. Its melody lacks the sweeping melismas of the W1 setting. Ma 288 matches Assisi 695, elaborating Agnus 267 with a similar, although even simpler, melody but with heightened neumes. Three other manuscripts transmit related versions, with slight variations: Ma 289, PBN 10508, and PBN 10511. The melodies in these five manuscripts constitute a trope family that contrasts with the setting in W1. A related setting, in regard to the source chant at least, is the three-part *Agnus Lux lucis* that appears in Fascicle VIII of W1 (fol. 93v). This version is very different melodically from the monophonic trope. The lowest, comparatively slow-moving line bears no melodic similarity to W1's Agnus 136, and the vocal gestures in the upper two voices are similar to each other, but different from the monophonic version. Although there are many melismas in the upper two voices, they consist mainly of two to five notes, with the exception of the last syllable of each phrase, which contains more extended passages. Even in these passages, however, the groups of currentes are not more than five, in contrast to the longer runs of eight or more found in the tenth fascicle.

In addition to the Agnus 267 elaborations, two other Agnus chants feature among the W1 trope concordances. The *Agnus Lux lucis* settings in PBN 1235 and PBN 9449 elaborate Schildbach Agnus 208, accompanied by an entirely different trope melody that is primarily syllabic.[34] Its melodic ideas seem even farther away from the style of W1. *Lux lucis* appears a total of three times in both manuscripts, each time with the same melody.[35] A fourth Agnus chant was apparently used for at least one version of *Agnus Vulnere quorum*; it is difficult to evaluate all settings because many of its concordant manuscripts are incomplete in some way,[36] or use imprecise music notation.[37] PBN 3126, the most informative concordance, contains the parent chant incipit and the first two words "Vulnere quorum" at the bottom of folio 77v, but the following folio with the remainder of the piece has been torn from the manuscript. Although only a portion of the trope survives, it is enough to make the following observations: the heightened neumes convey a fourth parent melody and a trope fragment that differs from W1 while sharing similar, but shorter, melodic gestures. This Agnus melody seems unlike any in Schildbach's catalog. If forced, the line could be categorized as a transposition of Agnus 136, but the variations are significant enough that the chant should be classified independently.

In conclusion, it can be summarized that none of the concordant Agnus tropes have the same parent melody as W1, with the possible exceptions of the *Agnus Vulnere quorum* in SL HB I.95, notated imprecisely in campo aperto, and the *Agnus Lux lucis* in Iv 60, which lacks music notation.[38] In addition to

W1's Agnus 136, there are three other Agnus melodies associated with the repertoire of texts. The Sanctus concordances, on the other hand, all stem from Sanctus 49. These findings suggest that the Sanctus tropes are firmly associated with a single parent chant, while the Agnus tropes need not necessarily rely on a single Agnus melody. It is also significant that concordances for both the Sanctus and Agnus texts have a range of different melodies with varying degrees of ornamentation, but by far, the most melismatic and virtuosic belong to W1. Most importantly, all twelve Fascicle X trope melodies can now be described as unica, confirming that the W1 collection is indeed remarkable.

Analysis

Looking first at the poetry alone, most of the trope lines have internal rhyme, which subdivides each line into two halves. This feature is true of all of the Sanctus tropes, whereas the Agnus tropes are varied, with some lines rhyming internally like the Sanctus tropes,[39] one remaining undivided,[40] and yet others rhyming internally not only within one line, but also with internal sections of other lines.[41] *Agnus Vulnere quorum* (no. 15) divides into not just two, but three sections per line. In the Sanctus tropes, all of the rhymes are bisyllabic, with the exception of the active present participle ("-ans") in *Sanctus Cunctorum dominans* (no. 7). In contrast, only two of the Agnus tropes have polysyllabic rhyme (nos. 10 and 14), while four match vowel sounds only in the last syllable. The latter rhyme technique is much more subtle to the ear. Also subtle is the prevalent use of alliteration.[42]

In both the Sanctus and the Agnus tropes, there are texts that rhyme with other lines of trope, and texts that rhyme with lines of the parent chant. The relationship of the original text to the trope text is interesting because although the untroped Ordinary texts are not meant to be poetry by themselves, they become the poetic framework for the tropes. Most often, the parent remains an external frame, but in a few places, the new text blends with the old. See, for example, how the words "Sanctus" and "excelsis" become part of the trope rhymes in *Sanctus Sanctus ab eterno* (no. 9). Most of the trope lines elaborate or continue the preceding line of parent chant text. In the Sanctus tropes, there are four trope insertions. The first three expand on the opening invocation by inserting additional characteristics of God after each "Sanctus,"[43] while the fourth is usually a freestanding sentence between the "Dominus deus" and "Benedictus" sections. The exceptions to this pattern are *Sanctus Omnia qui libras* (no. 6), which creates complete sentences after each "Sanctus"; *Sanctus Cunctorum dominans* (no. 7), which has no trope between "Dominus deus" and "Benedictus"; and *Sanctus Rex qui cuncta regis* (no. 5), which introduces a fragment that leads into the "Benedictus." The Agnus tropes are created by weaving three elaborations into the parent chant. Each of the three invocations "Agnus dei qui tollis peccata mundi" is expanded with additional characteristics of Jesus, inserted mid-sentence before the closing supplication "Miserere nobis" or "Dona nobis pacem." One variation on this pattern occurs in the third trope phrase of *Agnus Vulnere quorum* (no. 15), which elaborates on "Agnus dei," but also leads into "Dona nobis pacem."

Musically, the tropes are generally guided by the musical features of the parent chants (see "Tropes: Parent Chants" above). They all end on G. The *finalis*, the medieval theorists tell us, is the most important indicator of melodic mode; thus all of the trope melodies are in G (tetrardus) mode. Further, the majority of them include the concluding cadential formula A–B–A–A–G, an ending that is separated from previous notes by a tractus (a vertical line in the staff delineating groupings or signifying a rest), which in turn is preceded by a precadential melodic formula. The precadence formulae vary; some exhibit slight modification, while others have almost mutated into new passagework entirely. Internal phrases likewise end on G with one exception; the third trope phrase of *Sanctus Sanctus ab eterno* (no. 9) rests on the fifth above, a preferred note of the authentic mode.

Internal cadences are especially important in the tropes because they determine how the chant and the tropes connect. Table 2 illustrates the first and last pitches of each phrase, demonstrating how the trope lines link with the first and last notes of the chant phrases. Note that the Sanctus parent chant phrases all begin and end on the G *finalis*, whereas the Agnus phrases begin and end on B in addition to G. Without exception, initial trope phrases begin on G, while internal phrases commonly begin on C, D, or F, as well as G. When we look at how the parent chant and trope phrases interconnect, we realize that chant phrases ending on B are so frequently followed by F that the tritone leap is not a mistake. It is likely that in these cases F is considered an ornamental tone leading to G, and therefore poses no problem.[44]

Table 3 shows the melodic ranges of each of the tropes and their parent chants. The ambitus of the PBN 1112 Sanctus is an octave (d–d'), precisely the plagal melodic range of Hypomixolydian. Three of the Sanctus tropes also dip down to d, but they ascend further into the typical authentic range, reaching g' and even above: *Sanctus Christe yerarchia* (no. 4), *Sanctus Rex qui cuncta regis* (no. 5), and *Sanctus Omnia*

xiv

TABLE 2
Trope Phrase Analysis

Melody	Initial and Closing Pitch of Trope Insertions and Surrounding Parent Chant Segments			
Sanctus	Section I	Section II	Section III	Section IV
Sanctus Christe yerarchia	*g–g* g–g	*g–g* f'–g	*g–g* g–g	*g–g* f'–g *g–g*
Sanctus Rex qui cuncta regis	*g–g* g–g	*g–g* c'–g	*g–g*	*g–g* f'–g *g–g*
Sanctus Omnia qui libras	*g–g* g–g	*g–g* f'–g	*g–g* g–g	*g–g* g–g *g–g*
Sanctus Cunctorum dominans	*g–g* g–g	*g–g* c'–g	*g–g* f'–g	*g–g* g–g
Sanctus Condita de nichilo	*g–g* g–g	*g–g* c'–g	*g–g* d'–g	*g–g* f'–g *g–g*
Sanctus Sanctus ab eterno	*g–g* g–g	*g–g* c'–g	*g–g* d'–d'	*g–g* f'–g *g–g*
Agnus	Section I	Section II	Section III	
Agnus Archetipi mundi	*g–b* g–g *b–g*	*g–b* c'–g *b–g*	*g–b* f'–g *b–g*	
Agnus Pectoris alta	*g–b* g–g *b–g*	*g–b* g–g *b–g*	*g–b* f'–g *b–g*	
Agnus Qui de virgineo	*g–b* g–g *b–g*	*g–b* f'–g *b–g*	*g–b* g–g *b–g*	
Agnus Lux lucis	*g–b* g–g *b–g*	*g–b* d'–g *b–g*	*g–b* f'–g *b–g*	
Agnus Humano generi	*g–b* g–g *b–g*	*g–b* f'–g *b–g*	*g–b* c'–g *b–g*	
Agnus Vulnere quorum	*g–b* g–g *b–g*	*g–b* g–g *b–g*	*b–b* f'–g *b–g*	

Notes. Roman numerals above the music staves correspond to the sections in this table. Within each section, italic type shows the parent chant melody; roman represents the intertwined trope. The parent chants are based on PBN 1112.

qui libras (no. 6) exemplify a mixed mode combining both the authentic and plagal ranges. The second three Sanctus tropes have a narrower range, a ninth or a tenth, and would be classified as standard authentic mode plus a tone on either side. Of course, when the tropes are performed in their entirety, with parent chants and added phrases combined, the lowest note in all the works extends down to d and the range expands beyond the typical limit of a single modal category.

The Agnus chant of PBN 1112 has a moderate range, a seventh that spans from the subfinal f to a sixth above the final. Since this chant melody fills neither the authentic nor the plagal ranges completely, its mode must be determined by a means other than ambitus. A precursory examination of melodic characteristics, such as the absence of emphasis on the fifth above the final, suggests a plagal classification of the chant. The Agnus tropes have a wider range than the chant itself. Like their Sanctus counterparts, some of the tropes reach up through the authentic ambitus, and others expand further into both authentic and plagal ranges.

Comparison of all twelve tropes reveals an average range of an eleventh and full use of the authentic range. Although many of the tropes dip into the plagal range, their tessituras remain primarily authentic; sovereignty of the authentic over the plagal also dictates that the mixed range tropes be classified as authentic. Thus, in spite of the fact that the source chants

TABLE 3
Ambitus of the Parent Chant and Trope Melodies

Melody	Ambitus
Sanctus PBN 1112	d–d'
Sanctus Christe yerarchia	d–a'
Sanctus Rex qui cuncta regis	d–b'
Sanctus Omnia qui libras	d–g'
Sanctus Cunctorum dominans	f–a'
Sanctus Condita de nichilo	f–a'
Sanctus Sanctus ab eterno rex	f–g'
Agnus PBN 1112	f–e'
Agnus Archetipi mundi	e–g'
Agnus Pectoris alta	d–g'
Agnus Qui de virgineo	d–g'
Agnus Lux lucis	f–a'
Agnus Humano generi	d–g'
Agnus Vulnere quorum	d–g'

are plagal by themselves, the combination of chant and trope is tetrardus authentic, Mixolydian.

Rhythm

Although the pitch values are relatively clear, the rhythmic values in Fascicle X are uncertain. Many of the other fascicles of W1 illustrate sections or complete compositions in modal rhythm. The ligature combinations of the rhythmic modes, set apart by tracti, form rhythmic conventions recognized by the medieval musician.[45] However, at least to the modern eye, modal notation is often less than clear, as illustrated in the other W1 fascicles: interruptions of and variations in ligature patterns often occur in order to accommodate note divisions, text underlay, or scribal idiosyncrasies.[46] Modal notation seems to be the synthesis of a broader, more flexible, and varied practice. Fascicle X itself does not show consistent modal groupings upon immediate inspection, and thus the question of note values requires a closer look.

The conductus, because of their syllabic nature, do not provide much in the way of definitive rhythmic notation since the single noteheads required for syllabic text setting are ambiguous. Ruth Steiner, in her study of the related monophonic conductus in manuscript F, concludes that the rhythm there is not clear: elements of mode 1 or mode 5 are present in syllabic passages, while the melismas are indistinct, but not modal.[47] The melismatic tropes have more opportunities for ligature patterns to emerge, but it is uncertain whether such patterns convey rhythmic value in monophonic contexts.

From this time period, we find many writers discussing rhythm in the context of new polyphonic genres. Can relevant information about monophonic rhythm be drawn from these sources? Johannes de Garlandia, one of the first theorists writing about the Notre Dame tradition (ca. 1260), differentiates mensurable polyphony from "plainchant, which is unmeasured."[48] Franco of Cologne also distinguishes polyphony, as measured music, from plainchant, as unmeasured music, in his *Ars cantus mensurabilis* (ca. 1280):

> Mensurable music is melody measured by long and short time intervals. To understand this definition, let us consider what measure is and what time is. Measure is an attribute showing the length and brevity of any mensurable melody. I say "mensurable" because in plainsong this kind of measure is not present.[49]

Johannes de Grocheo, writing ca. 1300, conveys a similar definition but clarifies that *musica plana* is not completely without measure:

> Others divide music into plain or unmeasured music and measured, understanding by plain or unmeasured ecclesiastical, which was organized by Gregory in many tones. By measured they understand that which is made by different sounds measured and sounding at the same time, just as in conductus and motets.... But if they understand by unmeasured music something measured by no scale, they in reality are completely mistaken in their proferred [*sic*] opinion, since any practicality of music and of any art ought to be measured by the rules of that art. If however, by unmeasured they mean not too precisely measured, this division, as will be seen, can stand.[50]

Thus, in agreement with Garlandia and Franco, Grocheo explains that polyphonic conductus and motets are rhythmic, while *musica plana* is not as precisely measured.

The question remains, though, whether the Fascicle X material can be considered unmeasured plainchant.[51] The unadorned Ordinary texts are plainchant, certainly, but what about the newly interwoven material? Upon close inspection, I was able to locate some passages in Fascicle X that resemble Garlandia's modal rhythms. *Sanctus Christe yerarchia* (no. 4), for example, in the middle of the word "Christe," illustrates one such passage that could be interpreted modally (see facsimile of fol. 185v, end of line 9). The ligature pattern here is a three-note group followed by a series of two-note groups, the classic ligature combination for first mode. It seems that in addition to unmeasured passages, there are also passages in the W1 tropes that contain elements of modal rhythm. The fact that Fascicle X is nestled in the same manuscript with Notre Dame's polyphony, written by the same scribe(s), and most likely sung by the same cantors, poses a related question: might Fascicle X contain elements of polyphonic rhythmic notation, but for a single voice?[52]

The Notre Dame theorists discuss rhythm in the context of discantus, copula, and organum. The first genre, discant, is described as "the sounding together of various different voices according to mode and *equipollentia* of equivalent voices" (Garlandia),[53] and "the concordance of certain diverse melodies," tempus against tempus (Anonymous IV).[54] Thus, the primary characteristics of discant are (1) polyphonic, and (2) modal, with rhythmic equivalence between voices. Since discant is so completely dependant on the interrelationship of multiple voices, it does not hold much in common with W1, Fascicle X.

The next polyphonic genre, copula, does bear some similarity to Fascicle X. According to Garlandia:

> *Copula* is said to be that which is between discant and organum. The *copula* is described in another way: *copula* is that which proceeds to a unison by means of *equipollentia* with *rectus modus*. It is described in another way: there is a *copula* wherever a great number of *puncti* are written. A *punctus*, as the term is used here, is wherever there is a great number of *tractus* . . . and each part contains a great number of species, such as unisons or whole-tones, in one voice, according to an arranged number in proper order.[55]

xvi

This passage characterizes copula as having modal rhythm (*equipollentia* with *rectus modus*), sectionalization (*puncti*), and melodic sequence (species in an arranged number and proper order). Another Notre Dame theorist, the Anonymous of St. Emmeram (in *De musica mensurata*, ca. 1279), likewise states that copula is modal and sectional in defined succession.[56] Anonymous IV describes copula similarly: sharing characteristics of organum and discant, containing melodic sequence, with upper parts in modal rhythm.[57]

As I searched Fascicle X for these characteristics of copula, I found melodic sequences immediately. A good example is the sequential phrase on the melisma "celo" in the trope *Sanctus Christe yerarchia* (no. 4). (See facsimile of fol. 186r, beginning of line 9.) The sequential group illustrated in this example consists of a four-note ligature plus a four-note virga-currente combination that repeats seven times, descending stepwise. Clearly, the trope does contain the copula characteristic of sequential melody, but how does it compare rhythmically? The ligature groupings on "celo" do not readily lend themselves to a modal rhythm: the ligature combinations of 4–4–4–4 etc., even when subdivided into other combinations, would have to be forced in order to conform to one of the standard modal rhythm patterns.

This *Sanctus Christe yerarchia* example also illustrates a use of tracti that is different from the theorists' description for copula. Modal notation requires a system of tracti that divide the prescribed sets of ligatures (ordines) with rests, without regard for syllables or musical form. However, the tracti found in W1, Fascicle X, are not used in this fashion. In general, the tracti are placed in the staff, drawn though approximately one space, and part of the adjacent lines, in the location where the musical phrase has just been completed. They do not occur with prescribed regularity, although their placement is very logical. They are present as visual clarification, most often for text underlay, but also as a grouping device for beginnings and ends of sequential phrases and poetic sections. In *Sanctus Christe yerarchia*, the first tractus of folio 186r, line 8, marks the beginning of the word "cherubin," while the second and third mark the placement of the last syllable of the word. The next tractus comes at the end of the line, sectioning off the end of the sequential passage over "dat cantica." Likewise, the next tractus occurs at the end of a sequence on line 9, this time in the middle of the word "celo." Similarly, the first two tracti of the last line neatly mark off the placement of the last syllable, "-lo," of "celo," while the next two separate the section of plainchant, "Dominus deus sabaoth." In conclusion, then, the extended sequential, melismatic passages of the W1 tropes compare to copula with the fundamental ingredient of sequence, but the tropes differ by the absence of modal rhythm and an organizational use of tracti.

Contemporary writings on the third Notre Dame polyphonic genre, *organum purum*, further clarify the nuances of modal rhythm. Garlandia describes organum in the context of rhythmic performance:

> In *organum* the longs and breves are distinguished in this way, namely by consonance, by the figures (manner of notation), and by the rule of the penultimate. Whence the rule: whatever occurs by virtue of consonance is said to be long.
>
> Another rule: whatever is written as a long during the organum and before a rest is said to be long.
>
> Another rule: whatever occurs before a long-rest or before a perfect consonance is said to be long.[58]

Garlandia's comments indicate that in organum it is note placement, shape, and consonance, and not modal patterns, that determine how long a note is to be held.

Anonymous IV agrees that *organum purum* is not modal. He writes in his sixth chapter that, because of the rhythmic irregularities, this style of organum (described here as *organum in duplum*) cannot be set in three parts, as the rhythm is too free to accommodate a third melody line:

> And there is a sixth volume of organum in duplum like "Iudea et Ierusalem" and "Constantes," which indeed never occurs in triplum nor can occur that way on account of a certain mode of its own which it has that is different from the others, and because the longs are too long and the breves too short.[59]

Later in the treatise, he discusses what he calls irregular modes, note values that cannot fit into the molds of modal rhythm. His description of the seventh irregular mode includes a long elaboration of *organum purum*, which describes the ligature shapes:

> And in accordance with the seven gifts of the Holy Spirit is the seventh mode—most noble and worthy, more voluntary and pleasing. And this mode is a mixed and common mode, and it is made up of all the two-note ligatures mentioned above, and all the three-note ligatures, and all the four-note ligatures, etc. And properly speaking it is called pure and noble organum.... Also, *currentes* ... have a certain mode that is different from the others: it does not matter whether they are concordant or not, <but> descend quickly and as equally as possible.[60] (brackets original)

When I compared the organum descriptions above to Fascicle X, I found examples of the multiple ligature types, currentes, and combinations that Anonymous IV mentions. One such example is the word "israhelitas" from the trope *Sanctus Rex qui cuncta regis* (no. 5):

xvii

single notes, a three-note ligature, then three currentes with their preceding virga, another single virga followed by a two-note pes, a four-note ligature combined with an eight-note descending run, all written in the first third of the line (see facsimile of fol. 187r, line 1). This collection of note shapes looks like the nonmodal style that Anonymous IV describes as having "longs too long" and "breves too short." Thus, I would suggest that according to the Notre Dame theorists, note values in passages like this one should be determined by location and consonance. (See the following "Notes on Performance" for an application of these rules to monophony.)

In sum, it can be surmised that in places, the musical notation of W1, Fascicle X, is similar to the notation of plainchant, and is therefore unmeasured. Other passages resemble copula with extended sequential melismas. Still others prove similar to organum because of diverse ligature combinations, rendering them also nonmodal, with note length determined by such features as placement and consonance. However, in contrast to the predominance of unmeasured passages, there are also sections that contain elements of modal rhythm. These modal passages are infrequent and tend to be variations of two- and three-note ligatures that suggest either first or second mode.

Notes on Performance

The two contrasting genres of conductus and trope are quite similar when dealing with performance-related topics such as historical context, performing forces, phrasing, ornamentation, and the practical application of references to rhythmic modes. Although the conductus are musically simpler than the tropes, they contain similar nuances of ornamentation and text declamation. Because most of the musical notation does not convey specific rhythmic values (see "Rhythm" above), singers may wish to use poetic scansion, meter, and rhetoric as guides for performance of the predominantly syllabic conductus. The more elaborate music of the conductus, which occurs in strategically placed melismas, plays a significant structural role by helping singers declaim key points of the poetic structure. Melismatic caudae commonly serve as endings in the conductus repertoire of this period, and the W1 chants often feature opening melismas as well, usually on a syllable of exclamation or invocation. Both elaborations add important punctuation by framing a verse.

The tropes have an added layer in performance: it is important to bear in mind that a musical trope is a new interpolation, an insertion, added to preexisting chant. To make a mass more elaborate, for example, the lead cantor might select one trope from the many included in W1, as an ornament to the regularly sung Sanctus for the day. Tropes can take the form of textual additions, musical additions, or a combination of new music and text. As I have discussed previously, the tropes of W1, Fascicle X, add both new music and text together. They are important in that they add new meaning and beauty to the Sanctus and Agnus Dei. Everyone at the time would have been familiar with the untroped chants. In the absence of specific records illuminating the performance traditions of St. Andrews priory, I have drawn upon the next closest tradition, Notre Dame of Paris.

The question of note values in performance must be addressed, for although brief passages may be interpreted in first or second rhythmic mode according to the ligature groupings, the majority of the music follows other guiding factors. Anonymous IV discusses Notre Dame performance practice in the context of his discussion of organum. Even though he is writing about a polyphonic medium, his guidelines for the performance of relatively free rhythm, which disregards the ligature groupings necessary for modal notation, are relevant for other medieval genres:

> In *organum purum* the longs and breves [longs and shorts] are recognized by many different ways and methods. One way is as follows: every first note, whether it is a concordant note in one of the aforementioned concords or not, will either be a *longa parva* or a *longa tarda* or a *[longa] media*, whatever ligature it appears in, whether a two-note ligature or a three-note ligature, etc.[61]

In other words, the first note of a section should be a long note regardless of the written note shape or the harmonic interval. This long note is apparently relative, as he says it can be of short, long, or medium duration. He continues to stress that rhythm is determined by placement or concords, amplifying and clarifying with multiple examples:

> Also every last note will be long. . . . Also every penultimate note before a long rest . . . is long. . . . Also, for every note in a two-note ligature: the first, if it is in a concord, is long; if it is in a discord it is short. . . . Also for every last note in two-note ligatures: if it is concordant, it is long; if it is discordant, it is short. . . . Also, for every note of three-note ligatures: the first is long if it is in a concord. . . . For every note of a four-note ligature: the first or second or third or fourth are long in a concord, short in a discord.[62]

This passage can be summarized as saying that last notes and penultimate notes, in addition to the first notes already mentioned above, should be long, while every other type of note is long if concordant, and short if discordant. Concordant intervals are mentioned earlier in the treatise, where they are listed as octave, fifth, fourth, or unison, and sometimes major and minor third.[63]

At first, it may appear as if the concept of concords and discords is not applicable to monophony, but Anonymous IV's observations can in fact be applied to the W1 tropes. In single-line music, the intervals are heard silently against the melodic mode *finalis*. Since all of the Fascicle X tropes are in Mixolydian mode, with a *finalis* of G, they would all have the same relatively long and short notes according to Anonymous IV's observations: the more sustained notes would be G, C, D, and perhaps less long, the imperfect concord B. (Melodic passages between B and F are a normal occurrence in the context of G modes; thus, in general, the performer need not worry about avoiding the tritone by adding ficta.)

Anonymous IV gives further insight regarding note lengths in his explanation of currentes: "*Currentes* . . . have a certain mode that is different from the others: it does not matter whether they are concordant or not, [but] descend quickly and as equally as possible."[64] This passage is especially applicable to the W1 tropes, as they contain many sections with multiple groups of currentes. According to Anonymous IV, these runs should be sung rapidly and evenly, something that would result in entire sections of the tropes moving with great speed. (There are only two instances of currentes that descend by leap rather than step, found in *Agnus Qui de virgineo* [no. 12], and *Agnus Vulnere quorum* [no. 15]. These could either be interpreted as an indication to move quickly and equally through those notes, or an abbreviation for a descending scale encompassing all pitches between and including the written notes.)

Many times, the currentes occur in extended sequential passages. Since the notation of these passages does not relay specific rhythmic values, the performer may wish to discover his own phrasing of the first element according to the criteria above, and then repeat that series of durations for subsequent figures, thereby creating a rhythmic cell to illustrate each member of the sequence. For passages containing modal rhythm, singers can gradually ease in and out of the rhythmic patterns, as the modality usually does not last for an entire phrase.

All elements of performance should be combined to promote the gesture of a phrase, creating a framework for the trope text, which ultimately illuminates the parent chant. Points of rest fall where the text finishes a thought or sentence, and musical and poetic rhyme should be made subtly clear for the listener. The thirteenth-century singer's manual *Summa musice* advises composers to "establish pauses in the chant where the text itself requires a moment of pause."[65] The relative speed of some phrases, given the amount of music that falls between some syllables of text, should be quite quick so the listener does not lose track of the original word. At the same time, the larger gestures should flow slowly and in a stately fashion. Grocheo says that the Sanctus should be performed with fervent charity, ornate and slow at the same time.[66]

Grocheo's mention of the ornate may refer to quick notes such as currentes, but it may also include other figures from a palette of medieval ornamentation. Many passages in the W1 tropes contain what appear to be written-out ornamentation or improvisation. For example, the repeated notes at the beginning of many phrases may be an example of the technique that Garlandia calls *comminutio*, a repercussive ornament on one pitch.[67] The performance of repeated notes is also mentioned by Anonymous IV, who talks about ornaments that are not necessarily notated. He says that two notes on the same pitch represent an ornament called the *longa florata*, while the *duplex longa florata* is a single, long-note version of the *longa florata*, placed at the beginning of a section.[68] This *duplex longa florata* may be that which is suggested in many places in W1, Fascicle X, by notes penned with a long stroke. These are often initial notes, often dissonant, but not entirely restricted to phrase beginnings. The fact that the elongated notes in W1 are not limited to phrase beginnings suggests that Anonymous IV's *longa florata* (repeated notes) and *duplex longa florata* (elongated note) are two methods of notating a similar ornament.

Although Anonymous IV does not elaborate on the technical performance of the *longa florata*, Jerome of Moravia, in his thirteenth-century observations on French ecclesiastical music, does refer to vocal *flos harmonicus* (harmonic flowers). He describes three types of flowers, "long," "open," and "quick," organizing them in terms of speed and pitch: "long" flowers have a slow vibration, not exceeding a semitone; "open" flowers have a slow vibration, not exceeding a tone; and "quick" flowers have an accelerating vibration, not exceeding a semitone.[69] Jerome's first two flowers can be understood in terms of a modern trill, vibrated slowly and not exceeding a tone or a semitone (and possibly containing other small, nonstandard intervals), while the "quick" flower may be understood as an accelerating narrow trill or vibrato.[70] Jerome also discusses two more related ornaments: the *reverbratio* (possibly a rapid, smooth repercussion of a single pitch, like the baroque *trillo*) and the *procellaris* (probably a light, slow, narrow vibrato). The *reverbratio* seems to have the special function of an anticipation or appoggiatura when preceding a flower.[71] Today's singer may wish to carefully consider his performance choices for repeated notes (*longa florata*) and elongated notes (*duplex longa florata*) according to the treatises.

Further nuance, perhaps on a smaller scale, is suggested by the frequency of the *nota plicata* in W1. The plica indicates a change of pitch but also implies subtlety by virtue of its liquescence. The second note is often treated as a passing tone, and according to Lambertus (Pseudo-Aristotle), it should be sung by "the partial closing of the epiglottis combined with a subtle repercussion of the throat."[72] In syllabic music, this is often interpreted by vocalizing through a consonant, but here in Fascicle X, the plica is most often notated in the middle of a melisma, calling for a somewhat different interpretation. The plica sung mid-melisma is perhaps a subtle articulation of the tone by closing the epiglottis on the vowel.

The nuance and attention to detail required to execute the elaborate series of ornamental currentes in the Fascicle X tropes affirms a soloistic style. However, the term "soloist" in this context could signify one singer or a group of tightly woven specialists, as explained in *Summa musice*: "Monophonic chant [is] called monophonic (simplex) because it is either sung by one or by many in one manner."[73] Organum, the polyphonic genre most closely related to the tropes, has also been shown to be exclusively a soloistic art, involving from two to six singers.[74] In the medieval church, the choir would have sung the parent chant segments at the usual place within the liturgy, while the soloist(s) interspersed the trope elaborations. Modern musicians may wish to perform these tropes within the context of a reconstructed St. Andrews or Notre Dame mass, or choose an excerpted example to be sung in a modern concert setting. In either case, an awareness of the original liturgy is essential, and the performing forces of soloist and choir should be maintained.[75] In addition, the modern singer wishing to be true to the medieval performance context should pronounce the Latin text with an understanding of either medieval Scottish or medieval French influence.[76] Above all, I invite readers, performers, and audiences to appreciate the musical line, the sequential passages, the soaring flights at the top of the staff that gradually cascade down to the depths of the soul, the rhythmic nuance and florid ornaments, both written and implied, which grace statuesque foundations of chant, liturgy, and poetry.

Notes

1. In addition to W1, the principal manuscripts of the *Magnus Liber* are W2 and F; there are also a number of sources of smaller scope. See, for example, the manuscript listings in *Les quadrupla et tripla de Paris*, ed. Edward Roesner, Magnus Liber Organi, vol. 1 (Monaco: L'Oiseau-Lyre, 1993), lxxv–lxxx; and the concordant sources listed in *Les organa à deux voix du manuscrit de Wolfenbüttel, Herzog August Bibliothek, Cod. Guelf. 1099 Helmst.*, ed. Thomas Payne, Magnus Liber Organi, vol. 6 (Monaco: L'Oiseau-Lyre, 1996), lxxiii–lxxix. These sources hold some of the earliest written records of polyphonic music, some of the first music attributed to specific "composers" of polyphony, and the first attempts to notate and discuss rhythm.

2. Jacques Handschin made a good case for the entire codex having been written at or for St. Andrews in his "Zur Geschichte von Notre Dame," *Acta musicologica* 4 (1932): 5–17 and 49–55. In addition, the preface to Baxter's facsimile edition of W1 supported Handschin's belief that the early history of the manuscript was tied to St. Andrews, and it supplied further evidence that the codex was written in the first half of the fourteenth century. See *An Old St. Andrew's Music Book*, ed. J. H. Baxter (London: Humphrey Milford, 1931), vii–viii.

3. Heinrich Husmann used liturgical evidence to show that the original corpus of the *Magnus Liber*, W1 and F, was produced for the cathedral of Notre Dame in Paris. See his "The Origin and Destination of the *Magnus Liber Organi*," *Musical Quarterly* 49 (1963): 311–30. Rudolf Flotzinger also used liturgical evidence, making a convincing argument for a date of ca. 1265 in "Beobachtungen zur Notre-Dame-Handschrift W1 und ihrem 11. Faszikel," *Mitteilungen der Kommission für Musikforschung* 19 (1968): 245–62.

4. Edward Roesner concluded that the liturgical evidence pointed to St. Andrews more than any other house, and that the paleographic dating needed more study of Scottish or St. Andrews's scribal hands. He also ventured a connection between the appearance of W1 and the liturgical renaissance at St. Andrews after 1314. See Edward Roesner, "The Origins of W1," *Journal of the American Musicological Society* 29 (1976): 337–80. Five years later, Julian Brown provided Roesner's requested study of scribal hands, concluding that all the text of W1 is in the same hand, an intellectual French hand, written in the mid-thirteenth century (before 1250), while the marginalia are Scottish or English. In the same article, Sonia Patterson independently dated the flourished initials within the same time frame, ca. 1240, noting similarities to Scottish manuscripts, but she could not provide conclusive evidence about the provenance. Also at the same time, David Hiley examined concordances for the Ordinary chant along with melodic variants of sequences,

positing a thirteenth-century English musical tradition with Parisian contact. See Julian Brown, Sonia Patterson, and David Hiley, "Further Observations on W1," *Journal of the Plainsong and Mediaeval Music Society* 4 (1981): 53–80. More recently, Mark Everist presented evidence that the manuscript may have arrived in Scotland earlier than the dates suggested by the paleographic studies. Everist proposes that the circle of Guillaume Mauvoisin, bishop of St. Andrews (1202–38), may have been responsible for transmitting polyphonic repertoire from Paris to St. Andrews. See his "From Paris to St. Andrews: The Origins of W1," *Journal of the American Musicological Society* 43 (1990): 1–42.

5. Many further astute observations on the background of W1 have been made by Isobel Woods Preece and Warwick Edwards, who tie W1 to Scottish traditions and make important historical links. Yet even they call out for further study on W1's origins. See Isobel Woods Preece, *Our Awin Scottis Use: Music in the Scottish Church up to 1603*, ed. Sally Harper, Studies in the Music of Scotland (Glasgow: The Universities of Glasgow and Aberdeen, 2000).

6. The call number 677 is also associated with W1; 677 is the number that Otto von Heinemann assigns in his inventory of Wolfenbüttel manuscripts in *Die Handschriften der Herzoglichen Bibliothek zu Wolfenbüttel, Erste Abtheilung: Die Helmstedter Handschriften* (Wolfenbüttel, 1886), 2:87.

7. The most recent facsimile of W1 (*Die mittelalterliche Musik-Handschrift W1*, ed. Martin Staehelin, Wolfenbütteler Mittelalter-Studien, no. 9 [Wiesbaden: Harrassowitz, 1995]) provides a detailed physical description of the manuscript. Also see *Quadrupla et tripla*, ed. Roesner, lxxiii.

8. Bryan Gillingham, in *Indices to the Notre-Dame Facsimiles* (Ottawa: Institute of Mediaeval Music, 1994), does not list *Quomodo cantabimus* in W1, most likely because it is incomplete. He also includes "Ha quo serverite" as an additional composition between *Ve mundo a scandalis* and *In Rama sonat gemitus*, but this seems to be an oversight, as "Ha quo serverite" is the third strophe of *Ve mundo a scandalis*. The penultimate trope on fol. 191, *Agnus Humano generi*, is also missing from Gillingham's *Indices*.

9. The colophon text reads: "Qui liber est scriptus Walterus sit benedictus" (And this book is finished. May Walter be blessed). An even later hand has written "Ist" ("Iste") over the first word, "Qui," which would alter the first phrase of the translation: "The foregoing book is done." The music can be transcribed as:

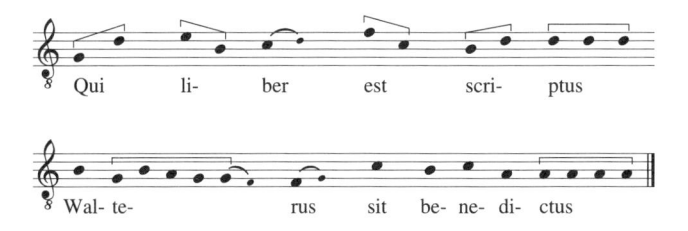

For more information on the colophon, see *Musik-Handschrift W1*, ed. Staehelin, 45; *St. Andrew's Music Book*, ed. Baxter; and Edward Roesner, "The Manuscript Wolfenbüttel, Herzog-August Bibliothek, 628 Helmstadiensis: A Study of Its Origins and of Its Eleventh Fascicle" (Ph.D. diss., New York University, 1974), 48–49. Julian Brown, in Brown, Patterson, and Hiley, "Further Observations," 57, believes the colophon was added before the middle of the fifteenth century in *cursiva secretary media*, using the *anglicana* form of *a*.

10. For illustrations showing how the fascicle fits into the entire manuscript, see *Musik-Handschrift W1*, ed. Staehelin, 9–15.

11. Edward Roesner has been able to distinguish scribes by fascicle, ascertaining that Scribe A wrote Fascicles I–V and VIII–X, Scribe B completed Fascicles VI and VII, and finally Scribe C added Fascicle XI. See Roesner, "Manuscript Wolfenbüttel," chap. 1; and *Quadrupla et tripla*, ed. Roesner, lxxiii–lxxiv. Julian Brown agrees that Fascicle XI is a later addition by a separate hand, but, admitting to the difficulties in distinguishing between nuances of script hands, sees Fascicles I–X as the work of a single scribe. See Brown, Patterson, and Hiley, "Further Observations," 55–58.

12. The one exception is folio 187, penultimate staff, which lacks a clef.

13. There is no indication that the ficta markings were not written by the original music scribe.

14. In the tropes, there are only descending plicae, which, in this case, appear to indicate stepwise motion. The conductus, however, also contain ascending plicae.

15. Anonymous IV, one of the leading music theorists and observers of the Notre Dame School and the *Magnus Liber*, discusses currentes in the context of modal and free rhythms throughout his treatise. See especially chap. 1–2 and 6 in Jeremy Yudkin, trans. and ed., *The Music Treatise of Anonymous IV: A New Translation*, Musical Studies and Documents, vol. 41 (Neuhausen-Stuttgart: American Institute of Musicology, 1985).

16. Ruth Steiner provides further insight into the satire of *Quomodo cantabimus*, as well as other satirical poetry and sermons from Paris in "Some Monophonic Latin Songs Composed around 1200," *Musical Quarterly* 52 (1966): 56–70.

17. See the edition of the motet *Quomodo cantabimus* in *Polyphonic Music of the Fourteenth Century*, vol. 1, ed. Leo Schrade (Monaco: L'Oiseau-Lyre, 1956), 51–53; and also the new notes and introduction by Edward Roesner in *Polyphonic Music of the Fourteenth Century*, vol. 1, ed. Leo Schrade, repr. (Monaco: L'Oiseau-Lyre, 1984).

18. F gives three notated strophes, but each strophe also has a second text, creating three double strophes. Hu contains an abbreviated version, with only one strophe. Two other manuscripts give the text only: Da provides three strophes (like W1) and Sab gives six (like F).

19. Regarding Philip the Chancellor, see Robert Falck, *The Notre Dame Conductus: A Study of the Repertory* (Ottowa: Institute of Medieval Music, 1981), 116. Falck also points out another medieval reference to *Ve mundo a scandalis* later in his text: the medieval grammarian John of Garland cites this piece in his *Ars rhythmica* (Falck, *Notre Dame Conductus*, 249).

20. For the purpose of this discussion, pitches will be named according to the method where c' = middle C when it is necessary to indicate octaves. It should be understood that medieval C clefs do not indicate absolute pitch.

21. From a slightly later time, Hu presents analogous notes from strophe 1 only, in a musical notation that has been described as both rhythmic and free. See editions of the Hu versions of *Ve mundo a scandalis* in *El codex musical de Las Huelgas*, ed. Higini Anglès (Barcelona: Institut d'Estudis Catalans, 1931), 1:351 and 3:385; and *The Las Huelgas Manuscript: Burgos, Monasterio de Las Huelgas*, ed. Gordon Anderson, Corpus Mensurabilis Musicae, vol. 79 (Neuhausen-Stuttgart: American Institute of Musicology, 1982), 2:xliv and 2:114. The rhythmic attributes of *Ve mundo a scandalis* are also discussed in Heinrich Husmann, "Ein Faszikel Notre-Dame-Kompositionen auf Texte des Pariser Kanzlers Philipp in einer Dominikanerhandschrift," *Archiv für*

Musikwissenschaft 24 (1967): 1–23; and Steiner, "Monophonic Latin Songs," 67–69.

22. Denis Stevens was one of the first to point out the bishop staff in the initial. See his "Music in Honor of St. Thomas of Canterbury," *Musical Quarterly* 56 (1970): 316–17. The following literature also specifically mentions *In Rama sonat genitus*: Jacques Handschin, "A Monument of English Polyphony," *Musical Times* 74 (1933): 697; Leonard Ellinwood, "The 'Conductus'," *Musical Quarterly* 27 (1941): 194; Leo Schrade, "Political Compositions in French Music of the 12th and 13th Centuries," *Annales musicologiques* 1 (1953): 16; and John Purser, *Scotland's Music: A History of the Traditional and Classical Music of Scotland from the Earliest Times to the Present Day* (Edinburgh: Mainstream, 1992), 52.

23. For further discussion about *In Rama sonat gemitus*'s historical setting and musical form, see Thomas Payne, "Datable 'Notre Dame' Conductus: New Historical Observations on Style and Technique," *Current Musicology* 64 (1998): 106–7; and Ellinwood, "Conductus," 194. Characteristics of the related monophonic Parisian sequence are detailed by Margot Fassler in "The Role of the Parisian Sequence in the Evolution of Notre-Dame Polyphony," *Speculum* 62 (1987): 345–74.

24. As an illustration, *Agnus Lux lucis* of W1, Fascicle X, has cues for each "Agnus dei," each "Miserere nobis," and "Dona nobis pacem." The three-part rendition of the same text on folio 84v, like most of the polyphonic tropes in the *Magnus Liber*, gives only the first "Agnus dei," proceeding through the trope text without further reference to the parent chant. One wonders about this scribal idiosyncrasy of Fascicle X: perhaps the virtuosity of the long melismas requires more cues in order to keep one's place.

25. For a brief description of PBN 1112 and its dates, see *The New Grove Dictionary of Music and Musicians*, 2nd ed. (hereafter *NG2*), s.v. "Sources, MS, § II, 7," by John Emerson/David Hiley, 841.

26. Peter Josef Thannabaur, ed., *Das einstimmige Sanctus der römischen Messe in der handschriftlichen Überlieferung des 11. bis 16. Jahrhunderts*, Erlanger Arbeiten zur Musikwissenschaft, no. 1 (München: Walter Ricke, 1962). This melody is also known as Vatican Sanctus melody 4.

27. Melody 49 is the second most commonly occurring melody out of the 231 melodies Thannabauer has compiled: 478 occurrences within 311 manuscripts. See the tables in Thannabauer, *Sanctus der römischen Messe*.

28. *Sanctus Christe yerarchia* contains the only written-out music for "sabaoth" in the W1 tropes. See the critical notes for *Sanctus Christe yerarchia* (no. 4).

29. See Martin Schildbach, "Das einstimmige Agnus Dei und seine handschriftliche Überlieferung vom 10. bis zum 16. Jahrhundert" (Ph.D. diss., Friedrich-Alexander-Universität, 1967), 117–19.

30. This melody is also known as Vatican Agnus melody 4. The "transposition" up a step does not retain the original configuration of tones and semitones of the F mode, but retains the relative melodic movement within the new mode. Interestingly, Schildbach lists many tropes for this transposition, demonstrating that it is not unusual.

31. SG 383 has a four line staff, with French square notation.

32. In fact, all concordances for this work are settings of the Sanctus. See "Critical Notes" in the critical report for a complete list of concordances.

33. The text of *Sanctus Omnia qui libras* is recorded with a third melody in St-M C, although some melodic gestures are similar to SG 383. In St-M C, the parent chant is more elusive: all three "Sanctus" incipits are left blank, but notes for "Dominus deus" do not correspond with Sanctus 49.

34. PBN 9449's notation is somewhat imprecise, written in campo aperto, but its neumes suggest the same melody as PBN 1235.

35. In PBN 1235, the third time is referenced by an incipit.

36. The *Agnus Vulnere quorum* trope of Assisi 695 has been mutilated with a large square excised from the beginning four staves of the trope. None of the parent melody is present, and the remaining portions of the trope melody differ from W1. Also incomplete, Li 2(17) has a blank four-line staff over the words of the entire trope.

37. The version in SL HB I.95 is written in Germanic neumes in campo aperto with uncertain pitch level. The source chant could be Agnus 136, as in W1, but this assessment is made based on the minimal cues in the setting: the neumes over the first two words.

38. It is acknowledged that this conclusion is preliminary; statistics may change when I am able to consult the additional *Lux lucis* manuscripts that were unavailable for the present study.

39. See *Agnus Pectoris alta* (no. 11), *Agnus Lux lucis* (no. 13), and the last line of *Agnus Archetipi mundi* (no. 10).

40. See *Agnus Humano generi* (no. 14).

41. See *Agnus Qui de virgineo* (no. 12), for example, where the internal rhyme scheme *bc* is found in lines 2, 5, and part of 8.

42. The rhyme schemes found in the tropes are highly reminiscent of medieval Celtic and Hiberno-Latin poetry. Possible Celtic connections are the subject of my current research.

43. *Sanctus Rex qui cuncta regis* (no. 5) only has two "Sanctus" elaborations.

44. In Purser, *Scotland's Music*, 56, Purser transcribes one small section of *Sanctus Christe yerarchia* as an illustration of medieval Scottish music. In two different places within the short example, he transposes the music up a third without explanation, inferring scribal error. His transposition removes some of the emphasis on the pitch F, perhaps in an effort to avoid tritone movement. However, the movement between B and F is quite common in the tropes. The original pitch level should thus be maintained.

45. Many studies have explored the features and problems of rhythmic modes: see, for example, Willi Apel, *The Notation of Polyphonic Music, 900–1600*, 5th ed. (Cambridge, Mass.: The Medieval Academy of America, 1953); *NG2*, s.v. "Rhythmic modes," by Edward Roesner; Roesner, "Manuscript Wolfenbüttel"; and *Quadrupla et tripla*, ed. Roesner.

46. Roesner concludes that we cannot know the exact rhythms of much of the Notre Dame repertoire, and that all the genres require flexibility in performance. He also indicates that many passages have multiple "correct" interpretations. See Edward Roesner, "The Emergence of *Musica mensurabilis*," in *Studies in Musical Sources and Style: Essays in Honor of Jan LaRue*, ed. Eugene Wolf and Edward Roesner (Madison: A-R Editions, 1990), 41–74; and *Quadrupla et tripla*, ed. Roesner, lxxxvii.

47. Steiner, "Monophonic Latin Songs."

48. Johannes de Garlandia, *De mensurabili musica*, trans. Stanley Birnbaum as *Concerning Measured Music* (Colorado Springs: Colorado College Music Press, 1978), 1.

49. Oliver Strunk, *Source Readings in Music History: Antiquity and the Middle Ages* (New York: Norton, 1965), 140.

50. Johannes de Grocheo, *De musica*, trans. Albert Seay as *Concerning Music*, 2nd ed. (Colorado Springs: Colorado College Music Press, 1973), 11.

51. The concordant manuscripts do not offer help in the deciphering of rhythm: none have the same trope melodies nor are they notated rhythmically.

52. Modal rhythms most likely arose as a function of polyphony. As two or more parts of music were sung simultaneously, it became more and more necessary to have ways of organizing the parallel lines. For descriptions of the birth of measured music, see Roesner, "Emergence of *Musica mensurabilis*"; and Ernest Sanders, "The Earliest Phases of Measured Polyphony," in *Music Theory and the Exploration of the Past*, ed. Christopher Hatch and David Bernstein (Chicago: University of Chicago Press, 1993), 41–58.

53. Charles Larkowski, "The *De musica mensurabili positio* of Johannes de Garlandia: Translation and Commentary" (Ph.D. diss., Michigan State University, 1977), 59.

54. Yudkin, *Anonymous IV*, 65.

55. Larkowski, *"De musica mensurabili positio,"* 110. See also Jeremy Yudkin, "The *Copula* According to Johannes de Garlandia," *Musica Disciplina* 34 (1980): 67–84.

56. The Anonymous of St. Emmeram also defines copula as between discant and organum and having the special voice quality of organum. See Jeremy Yudkin, "The Anonymous of St. Emmeram and Anonymous IV on the *Copula*," *Musical Quarterly* 70 (1984): 5–14.

57. See Yudkin's deductions on the copula according to Anonymous IV in his "Anonymous on the *Copula*"; and "Notre Dame Theory: A Study of Terminology, Including a New Translation of the Music Treatise of Anonymous IV" (Ph.D. diss., Stanford University, 1982), 96–97. A clear musical example of copula can be seen in *Alleluia Posui adiutorium* in F, folio 36v, at the end of system 1. This piece, cited as copula by Anonymous IV (Yudkin, *Anonymous IV*, 50 and 76), has been discussed in Charles Coussemaker, *L'art harmonique aux XIIe et XIIIe siècles* (Paris: Durand, 1865); Fritz Reckow, ed., *Der Musiktraktat des Anonymous 4*, Beihefte zum Archiv für Musikwissenschaft (Wiesbaden: Steiner, 1967), 1:103; and Yudkin, "Notre Dame Theory," 99.

58. Larkowski, *"Musica mensurabili positio,"* 111–12. Garlandia starts the discussion by explaining that organum is a general term for polyphony, as well as a specific term for the genre he is about to discuss (ibid., 111). He also explains that the specific *organum per se* proceeds according to *modus rectus* or *modus non rectus*, which he defines respectively as "that by which discant proceeds," and that which proceeds by "non recta measurement"; *organum non rectum* is what he is discussing in the passage quoted here. It is very likely that the organa he refers to as having *modus rectus* are *organum triplum* and *organum quadruplum*, as clarified by Anonymous IV in his differentiation between *organum triplum* and *organum duplum*. In the context of this edition, I will use *organum purum*, or *organum per se*, interchangeably with Garlandia's *organum non rectum*. (See Yudkin, *Anonymous IV*, 73.)

59. Yudkin, *Anonymous IV*, 73. Yudkin points out that Anonymous IV cannot mean that the piece *Iudea et Ierusalem* and its verse "Constantes" cannot occur in a three-voice arrangement, since there are three-voice versions in F and in W2. Yudkin, "Notre Dame Theory," 39.

60. Yudkin, *Anonymous IV*, 77–80. Fortunately, Anonymous IV does refer to an example of organum earlier in his treatise, *Iudea et Ierusalem*. This two-voice composition is found in the third fascicle of W1, folio 17 (also F, fol. 65r; and W2, fol. 47r), where currentes and the combinations of two-, three-, and four-note ligatures that Anonymous IV mentions can be easily recognized.

61. Ibid., 78.

62. Ibid.

63. Ibid., 62. Garlandia explains these in more detail as perfect concords: unison, octave; imperfect concords: major and minor thirds; in-between concords: fifths and fourths. See Garlandia, *De mensurabili musica*, trans. Birnbaum, 15–16.

64. Yudkin, *Anonymous IV*, 79.

65. *The "Summa musice": A Thirteenth-century Manual for Singers*, ed. Christopher Page (New York: Cambridge University Press, 1991), 120.

66. Grocheo, *De musica*, trans. Seay, 41.

67. See Timothy McGee, *The Sound of Medieval Song: Ornamentation and Vocal Style According to the Treatises* (Oxford: Clarendon Press, 1998), 72–79, for a discussion on repeated pitch ornaments.

68. Yudkin, *Anonymous IV*, 79.

69. [Jerome] Hieronymous de Moravia, *Tractatus de musica*, ed. Simon Cserba (Regensburg: Verlag Friedrich Pustet, 1935), 184. A translation of part of Jerome's chapter 25 can be found in Carol MacClintock, ed., *Readings in the History of Music in Performance* (Bloomington: Indiana University Press, 1979), 3–7. Also see McGee, *Sound of Medieval Song*, 63–67, for a translation and discussion of Jerome's harmonic flowers.

70. McGee wisely observes that Jerome's choice of language in describing the flowers as *not exceeding the limits* of a tone or semitone suggests that these vocal ornaments can include intervals other than our standard tone and semitone. See McGee, *Sound of Medieval Song*, 64.

71. Moravia, *Tractatus*, ed. Cserba, 185. See McGee's conclusions in McGee, *Sound of Medieval Song*, 68.

72. Lambertus (Pseudo-Aristotle), *Tractatus de musica*, as discussed in Apel, *Notation of Polyphonic Music*, 226–27.

73. *Summa musice*, ed. Page, 124.

74. Craig Wright, *Music and Ceremony at Notre Dame of Paris, 500–1550* (New York: Cambridge University Press, 1989), 342.

75. In the medieval cathedral of Notre Dame, the performing forces would have been all male. (See Wright, *Music and Ceremony*, 318–25.) However, the C clefs employed in the notation of W1, Fascicle X, do not convey anything other than relative pitch, and thus do not dictate vocal range or gender. It is conceivable that this or similar repertoire may have been sung in nunneries or other ecclesiastical settings where women would have been the trained soloists and choir. It is likely that the medieval performance traditions of sacred music did not involve mixed genders, however.

76. Harold Copeman, *Singing in Latin or Pronunciation Explor'd*, rev. ed. (Oxford: By the author, 1992), 135–38, gives information about the pronunciation of Scots-Latin, although his earliest examples are from much later in the sixteenth century. Also see chapters on Anglo-Latin (chap. 4) and French-Latin (chap. 6) in Timothy McGee, ed., with A. G. Rigg and David Klausner, *Singing Early Music: The Pronunciation of European Languages in the Late Middle Ages and Renaissance* (Bloomington: Indiana University Press, 1996).

Texts and Translations

In preparing the following edition, I have transcribed the texts from the facsimile and later checked them with the beautiful original codex in Wolfenbüttel. I have tried to respect the original texts but also to provide a form that is accessible to the modern reader. Each piece is laid out poetically, and for the tropes, the parent texts are supplied in italics to show how they intertwine with the new texts. The rhyme scheme is indicated below each text, and here again, the parent chant segments are represented by italics.

Common medieval abbreviations are expanded tacitly, while punctuation and spelling are left primarily as they appear in the manuscript. Because I have not added extra punctuation to the Latin text, readers will want to look to the parallel translations for insights on phrasing. I have distinguished between *u* and *v* according to modern use, as the scribe seems to use them interchangeably. Other nonstandard spellings (e.g., writing *i* for *j* as in "iusto," writing *e* for the diphthong *ae* as in "celi" and "rome," interchanging *y* and *i* as in "archetipi" and "ymago," and adding or omitting *h* before vowels as in "perhennis" or "[h]yperusya") are retained; one can often gather important clues about the flavor and pronunciation of the language from these idiosyncratic spellings. Spellings are corrected, with mention in the notes following the texts, only when they seem to result from scribal error. Capitalization has been standardized to include proper names when appropriate and the beginnings of sentences (i.e., words following a period) in the conductus. For the tropes, the edition follows the source in placing a capital letter at the beginning of each phrase of added text.

At times, it seems as if the scribe coloring the large initials, who did his job after the text scribe, overlooked some letters, and so there are a number of words that needed to be reconstructed. In addition, a large part of the parent chants are only represented in the manuscript with cues. Texts of the complete original Ordinary chants are expanded tacitly here, with notes recording any letters missing in the cues. Any other missing letters or words are supplied or expanded in brackets. The notes below each text describe any difference between the codex and the edition that I have not previously mentioned in the above editorial procedure.

In the preparation of the text, I have studied and compared all of the available concordant manuscripts (Assisi 695, Bar 1408/9, F, Fauv, Hu, Iv 60, Li 2[17], Ma 288, Ma 289, Ma 19421, OxB 775, PBA 135, PBN 1235, PBN 2298, PBN 3126, PBN 7185, PBN 9449, PBN 10508, PBN 10511, SG 378, SG 383, SG 546, SL HB I.95, and St-M C). Some of the information on concordant readings is relayed in modern catalogs, including Guido Maria Dreves, Clemens Blume, and Henry Marriott Bannister, eds., *Analecta hymnica medii aevi*, 55 vols. (Leipzig: Reisland, 1886–1922); and Gunilla Iversen, *Corpus Troporum VII: Tropes du Sanctus; Tropes de l'ordinaire de la messe*, Studia Latina Stockholmiensia, vol. 34 (Stockholm: Almqvist & Wiksell International, 1990). In the comments below, these collections are abbreviated as *AH* and *CT* VII respectively. The textual similarities are striking in the two conductus and the five tropes that have concordances. Most agree with the wording and placement; differences are mainly small and orthographic. These differences are explained in the notes to the texts.

1. Quomodo cantabimus

[Quomodo cantabimus
sub iniqua lege.
Oves quid attendimus.
Lupus est in grege.][1]

Decisis panniculis
nostris offert oculis
Ihesus inconsutilis
tunice cissuram[2]
suam iudex humilis
sustinet pressuram.

O quando discutiet
speluncam latronum
quam tremendus veniet
deus ultionum.

How shall we sing
under the unjust law?
Sheep, for what do we wait?
A wolf is in the flock.

In torn rags,
Jesus presents to our eyes
the tear of his
seamless tunic.
As a humble judge,
he wears his own affliction.

Oh, when will he scatter
the den of thieves?
How terrifying he comes,
the God of judgments.

Rhyme scheme. abab ccc′dc′d efef

Notes. **1.** Text is fragmentary because of the missing folios in W1. Text in brackets is from F, fol. 426v. **2.** The standard spelling is "scissuram," as written in F. It is interesting that Fauv transmits a similar spelling: "cisuram."

2. Ve mundo a scandalis

Ve mundo a scandalis
ve vobis[1] ut acephalis[2]
quorum libertas teritur
rome dormitat oculus[3]
cum sacerdos ut populus[4]
iugo servili[5] premitur.

[V]e quorum votis alitur
et pinquescit exactio
a quibus nulli parcitur
ut suo parcant[6] proprio
set in eos revertitur
sua tandem proditio
et fraus in se colliditur
iusto dei iudicio.

Ha quo se vertit vinea
qua recondet in fovea
fructus suos colonus[7]
cum pari mente sitiant[8]
ut labores diripiant
hinc pater hinc patronus.

Woe to the world for its stumbling blocks,
woe to you, as those without leaders,
whose freedom is worn away.
The eye of Rome sleeps
when the priest, like the people,
is weighed down by the yoke of servitude.

Woe to those whose debt-extraction is fed
and grows fat with offerings [of others].
[Woe to those] who spare no one;
those who would not even spare their own.
But nevertheless, their own treason
is turned back against them,
and their fraud is shattered upon them
by God's righteous judgment.

Ha! Where the vineyard [row] turns,
where in a pit the farmer
stores up his produce,
let those with such a mind go thirsty,
so that their labors may be scattered
this way by the elder, that way by the protector.

Rhyme scheme. aabccb bdbdbdbd eefggf

Notes. **1.** F and Hu have "nobis." **2.** Hu has "accephulis." **3.** Hu has "occulis." **4.** Hu has "poppulis." **5.** Hu has "servuli." **6.** Text is "parcat"; F supplies "parcant," which fits better grammatically. **7.** F has "calonus." **8.** Text is "sitiat."

3. In Rama sonat gemitus

In Rama sonat gemitus	In Rama, a cry rings out
plorante Rachel anglie.	while Rachel of England is weeping,
Herodis namque genitus	for a descendant of Herod
dat ipsam ignominie	gives her over to shame.
en eius primogenitus	Behold, her first-born,
et Ioseph cantuarie	the Joseph of Canterbury,
exulat[1] si sit venditus	lives in exile since he has been sold;
egiptum colit gallie.	he dwells in the Egypt of France.

Rhyme scheme.   abababab

Note.   **1.** The standard spelling is "exsulat."

4. Sanctus Christe yerarchia

Sanctus.	*Holy*
Christe[1] yerarchia	Christ, the high priest,
sabaoth deus yperusya.	God of Hosts, supreme being,
Sanctus.	*Holy*
Virtus vita via	strength, life, way,
patris perfecta sophia.	perfect wisdom of the Father,
Sanctus.[2]	*Holy*
Cui resonante melo	for whom, with resounding melody,
cherubin dat cantica celo.	the cherubim raise their songs to heaven,
Dominus deus sabaoth.	*Lord God of Hosts.*
Pleni sunt celi et terra gloria tua.	*Heaven and earth are full of your glory.*
Osanna in excelsis.	*Hosanna in the highest.*
Vox quorum tota	Of those whose combined voice
tibi psallat suscipe vota.	sings psalms to you, accept their offerings.
Benedictus qui venit in nomine domini.	*Blessed is he who comes in the name of the Lord.*
Osanna in excelsis.	*Hosanna in the highest.*

Rhyme scheme.   a bb a bb a cc d e f gg h f

Notes.   **1.** The scribe coloring the initials writes his symbol for "Chri-" with an upper case x at the beginning of the next staff, apparently without noticing that the text scribe had written the cue "pi" immediately after the "Sanctus" incipit, near the beginning of the first staff.   **2.** The scribe omitted the "Sanctus" before the third line of trope.

5. Sanctus Rex qui cuncta regis

Sanctus.	*Holy*
Rex qui cuncta regis	king, you who rule all things
iuste[1] moderamine legis.	with a government of righteous law,
Sanctus.	*Holy,*
Qui celo ditas	you who for heaven makes rich the Israelites,
quos eligis israhelitas.	whom you have chosen,
Sanctus.[2]	*Holy*
Dominus deus sabaoth.	*Lord God of Hosts.*
Pleni sunt celi et terra gloria tua.	*Heaven and earth are full of your glory.*
Osanna in excelsis.	*Hosanna in the highest.*
Ad nutum cuius	At whose command
rota mundi volvitur huius.	the wheel of this world is turned,
Benedictus qui venit in nomine domini.	*blessed is he who comes in the name of the Lord.*
Osanna in excelsis.	*Hosanna in the highest.*

Rhyme scheme.   a bb *a* cc *a d e b′ a′a′ f b′*

Notes.   **1.** SG 383, SG 378, *AH*, and *CT* VII all give "justo," although "juste" ("justae") can be translated correctly. "Juste" ("iuste") modifies "legis," whereas "justo" would modify "moderamine."   **2.** There would normally be a trope between the third "Sanctus" and the "Dominus deus." The concordances place W1's last trope phrase after the third "Sanctus," and a fourth line of trope before the "Benedictus"; the fourth line is given in SG 383, SG 378, *AH*, and *CT* VII. It is unknown whether the W1 version transmits an omission or a variation. In any case, any missing W1 music remains elusive, as the concordant texts have different melodies. Insertion of the concordant text gives the following poetic layout: "*Sanctus.* / Rex qui cuncta regis / iuste moderamine legis. / *Sanctus.* / Qui celo ditas / quos eligis israhelitas. / *Sanctus.* / Ad nutum cuius / rota mundi volvitur huius. / *Dominus deus sabaoth.* / *Pleni sunt celi et terra gloria tua.* / *Osanna in excelsis.* / Ad nos et rursum / rediens vehit agmina sursum. / *Benedictus qui venit in nomine domini.* / *Osanna in excelsis.*" The resulting rhyme scheme is *a* bb *a* cc *a* a′a′ *d e b′* ff *g b′*.

6. Sanctus Omnia qui libras

Sanctus.	Holy,
Omnia qui libras	you who holds all things in balance,
diademate[1] celica vibras.	you shimmer with the heavenly diadem.
Sanctus.	Holy,
Tu vergis celum	you bend the [arching] sky;
tu formidabile telum.	you [bend] the fearful weapon.[2]
Sanctus.	Holy,
Tu quatis arce patris	you strike from the Father's stronghold;
timor infernalibus atris.	[you are] a terror to the dark infernal realms.
Dominus deus sabaoth.	Lord God of Hosts,
Pleni sunt celi et terra gloria tua.	heaven and earth are full of your glory.
Osanna in excelsis.	Hosanna in the highest.
Mortales sacro	You bring mortals
trahis ad tua regna lavacro.	to your kingdom through holy cleansing.
Benedictus qui venit in nomine domini.	Blessed is he who comes in the name of the Lord.
Osanna in excelsis.	Hosanna in the highest.

Rhyme scheme.   a bb *a* cc *a* dd *e f d′* gg *h d′*

Notes.   **1.** St-M C, *AH*, and *CT* VII have "diademata."   **2.** Here the poet is likely drawing an allusion to bow and arrow.

7. Sanctus Cunctorum dominans

Sanctus.	Holy,
Cunctorum dominans	ruling all things,
sine meta cuncta gubernans.	guiding all things, without boundary,
Sanctus.[1]	Holy,
Equalis patri	equal to the Father,
confringens claustra baratri.	shattering the prison gates of the abyss,
Sanctus.	Holy
Spiritus alme tuo	nourishing Spirit,
replens pia pectora dono.[2]	you replenish pious hearts with your gifts.
Dominus deus sabaoth.	Lord God of Hosts,
Pleni sunt celi et terra gloria tua.	heaven and earth are full of your glory.
Osanna in excelsis.	Hosanna in the highest.
Benedictus qui venit in nomine domini.	Blessed is he who comes in the name of the Lord.
Osanna in excelsis.	Hosanna in the highest.

Rhyme scheme. a bb *a* cc *a* dd *e f g c' g*

Notes. **1.** The initial *S* is missing from the cue. **2.** Text is "dona"; however, "dono" rhymes with "tuo" and makes better syntax as an ablative of means. After "dona" ("dono"), the only other text and music given in W1 for this piece is the cue for "Benedictus," immediately following this third line of trope. At this point in the chant, however, one does not expect "Benedictus," but rather the cue "Dominus deus." One wonders whether the composition is transmitted in its complete form, with only three lines of trope, or whether the scribe might have left out a fourth line of troping. The other W1 compostions have four troped lines, thus the cue "Benedictus" seems early here.

8. *Sanctus Condita de nichilo*

Sanctus.	*Holy,*
Condita de nichilo	you who in your palm enclose all things,
qui claudis cuncta pugillo.	[things] created from nothing,
Sanctus.[1]	*Holy,*
Virginis absque patre	a virgin's offspring, apart from any father,
proles patris et sine matre.	of the Father, and without a mother,
Sanctus.	*Holy*
Spiritus utrique	Spirit, to each
consors et compar ubique.	a companion and coequal everywhere,
Dominus deus sabaoth.	*Lord God of Hosts.*
Pleni sunt celi et terra gloria tua.	*Heaven and earth are full of your glory.*
Osanna in excelsis.	*Hosanna in the highest.*
Vox pia servorum	The pious voice of [your] servants
conscendat ad astra polorum.	ascends to the stars of heaven.
Benedictus qui venit in nomine domini.	*Blessed is he who comes in the name of the Lord.*
Osanna in excelsis.	*Hosanna in the highest.*

Rhyme scheme. a bb *a* cc *a* dd *e f g* hh *i g*

Note. **1.** The initial *S* is missing from the cue. The first letters are also missing from the subsequent cues "Dominus" and "Benedictus."

9. *Sanctus Sanctus ab eterno*

Sanctus.	*Holy,*
Sanctus ab eterno	holy, from eternity,
rex regum iure superno.	King of kings by highest law,
Sanctus.[1]	*Holy,*
Sanctus labe carens	holy, free from blemish,[6]
quem parit alma parens.[2]	whom the nurturing mother brings forth,
Sanctus.[3]	*Holy,*
Sanctus amor patris	holy, love of the Father
et proles[4] et incola matris.	and offspring and inhabitant of a mother,
Dominus deus sabaoth.	*Lord God of Hosts.*
Pleni sunt celi et terra gloria tua.	*Heaven and earth are full of your glory.*
Osanna in excelsis.	*Hosanna in the highest.*
[Q]uem trinum triplicat	Whom deity triples as three,
deitas deus unus amicat.	God encompasses as one.
Benedictus[5] *qui venit in nomine domini.*	*Blessed is he who comes in the name of the Lord.*
Osanna in excelsis.	*Hosanna in the highest.*

Rhyme scheme. a bb *a* cc *a* dd *e f d'* gg *h d'*

Notes. **1.** The initial *S* is missing from the cue. **2.** Text is "patens" but should probably be "parens." **3.** The initial *S* is also missing from this cue. **4.** Text is "prolis," but "proles" seems more appropriate. **5.** The initial *B* is missing from the cue. **6.** "Blemish" could also be translated as "The Fall" (of Adam and Eve).

10. Agnus Archetipi mundi

Agnus dei qui tollis peccata mundi
Archetipi mundi stat[1] nutu cuius ymago.

Miserere[2] nobis.
Agnus dei qui tollis peccata mundi
[S]umma sophia noys[3] protopanton[4] prima propago.

Miserere nobis.
Agnus dei qui tollis peccata mundi
Binarii talis
   nexus individualis.[5]
Dona nobis pacem.

Lamb of God, you who takes away the sins of the world,
by whose command the image of the primeval world
   stands firm,
have mercy on us.
Lamb of God, you who takes away the sins of the world,
highest wisdom, mind, the first among all, the first
   offspring,
have mercy on us.
Lamb of God, you who takes away the sins of the world,
of such a twofold [nature],
   the bond is indivisible.
Grant us peace.

Rhyme scheme. a b c a b c a c'c' d

Notes. **1.** *CT* VII (*Sanctus Archetypi mundi*) has "stans"; SG 383 (*Sanctus Archetypi mundi*) has "stat." **2.** The initial *M* is missing from the cue. **3.** Text is "nobis," but SG 383 and *CT* VII give "noys." Because of the surrounding Greek words ("sophia," "protopanton"), "noys" seems the more likely, and more correct, reading. **4.** SG 383 (*Sanctus Archetypi mundi*) has "prothopanton." **5.** SG 383 (*Sanctus Archetypi mundi*) has "Binarii talis nexu non dividualis" as the third and last line of trope; *CT* VII (*Sanctus Archetypi mundi*) has "Spes pia sanctorum, pax, gloria, vita bonorum" as the third and last line of trope.

11. Agnus Pectoris alta

Agnus dei qui tollis peccata mundi
Pectoris alta rigans
   fons secula crimine purgans.[1]
Miserere nobis.
Agnus dei qui tollis peccata mundi
Omnia vis vegetans
   mortem moriendo relegans.
Miserere nobis.
Agnus dei qui tollis peccata mundi
[V]eniet nos dignans
   celo terrena resignans.[2]
Dona nobis pacem.

Lamb of God, you who takes away the sins of the world,
fountain watering the depths of the heart,
   cleansing the world of its sin,
have mercy on us.
Lamb of God, you who takes away the sins of the world,
strength enlivening all things,
   banishing death by dying,
have mercy on us.
Lamb of God, you who takes away the sins of the world,
he shall come,[3] making us worthy,
   transferring the things of this earth to heaven.
Grant us peace.

Rhyme scheme. a bb c a bb c a bb d

Notes. **1.** There is an abbreviation symbol at the end of the text, the end of folio 198v, that looks like a *t* with a curled crossbar. This often is an abbreviation for the passive verb ending "-tur," but in this case the letter *s* seems to make the most sense grammatically and poetically. **2.** Text is "resinans." **3.** In the process of adding text to the parent chant, the poet has not always perfectly aligned the verb forms; there is sometimes a dissonance between grammatical persons, as seen here.

12. Agnus Qui de virgineo

Agnus dei qui tollis peccata mundi
Qui de virgineo
   sumpsisti corpore corpus.
Miserere nobis.

Lamb of God, you who takes away the sins of the world,
who from a virgin's body
   took on his own body,
have mercy on us.

Agnus dei qui tollis peccata mundi	*Lamb of God, you who takes away the sins of the world,*
Et nostrum propitio	and by [your] propitious wound
sanasti vulnere vulnus.	you healed our wound,
Miserere nobis.	*have mercy on us.*
Agnus dei qui tollis peccata mundi	*Lamb of God, you who takes away the sins of the world,*
Lux et ymago	light and image of the Father,
patris verum de lumine lumen.	from light, true light,
Dona nobis pacem.	*grant us peace.*

   Rhyme scheme.   a bc d a bc d a be e'

13. Agnus Lux lucis

Agnus dei qui tollis peccata mundi	*Lamb of God, you who takes away the sins of the world,*
Lux lucis[1] verbumque patris	light of light and word of the Father
virtusque perhennis.[2]	and everlasting power,
Miserere nobis.	*have mercy on us.*
Agnus dei qui tollis peccata mundi	*Lamb of God, you who takes away the sins of the world,*
Verus sanctorum splendor	true glory of the saints
nosterque redemptor.	and our redeemer,
Miserere nobis.	*have mercy on us.*
Agnus dei qui tollis peccata mundi	*Lamb of God, you who takes away the sins of the world,*
Nostra[3] salus pax vera deus	our salvation, true peace, God,
altissima virtus.	the highest power,
Dona nobis pacem.	*grant us peace.*

   Rhyme scheme.   a bb b a cc b a dd e

   Notes.   **1.** PBN 10511 reads, "Lux lucis splendor verbumque patris," but "splendor" is crossed out.   **2.** *AH, CT* VII, and PBN 10508 have "perennis," while PBN 1235, PBN 3126, PBN 9449, PBN 10511, Iv 60, Ma 288, Ma 289, and Assisi 695 have "perhennis." **3.** Iv 60 has "Nostras."

14. Agnus Humano generi

Agnus dei qui tollis peccata mundi	*Lamb of God, you who takes away the sins of the world,*
Humano generi vitam cruce qui reparasti.	who by the cross restored life to human kind,
Miserere nobis.	*have mercy on us.*
Agnus dei qui tollis peccata mundi	*Lamb of God, you who takes away the sins of the world,*
[S]alva nos miseros rex qui bona cuncta creasti.	save us miserable ones; King, you who created all good things,
Miserere nobis.	*have mercy on us.*
Agnus dei qui tollis peccata mundi	*Lamb of God, you who takes away the sins of the world,*
Iungas nos superis qui sunt super astra locati.	you join us to those above, who are set above the stars.
Dona nobis pacem.	*Grant us peace.*

   Rhyme scheme.   a b c a b c a b' d

15. Agnus Vulnere quorum

Agnus dei qui tollis peccata mundi	*Lamb of God, you who takes away the sins of the world,*
Vulnere quorum[1]	for the wound of which
ledimur omnes	we all suffer,
infitiati.[2]	we deniers,
Miserere nobis.	*have mercy on us.*
Agnus dei qui tollis peccata mundi	*Lamb of God, you who takes away the sins of the world,*
Inviolate	the inviolate virgin's
virginis alme	nurturing offspring,
nate paterque.	[child] and Father,[4]

Miserere nobis.	*have mercy on us.*
Agnus dei qui tollis peccata mundi	*Lamb of God, you who takes away the sins of the world,*
Sanguinis unda	by the flow of your blood,
pectora munda	cleanse our hearts,
perpetuamque.[3]	and eternal[5]
Dona nobis pacem.	*peace give to us.*

Rhyme scheme.   a bca' c' a ddd c' a eed f

Notes.   **1.** SL HB I.95 has "mortis" instead of "quorum."   **2.** Li 2(17) and *AH* have "daemonis arte" instead of "infitiati"; Assisi 695 has a lacuna where the first four staves of notation are half cut out, but "-mur" from the end of "laedimur" and "om-" from the beginning of "omnes" remain, indicating that the text is probably the same or similar to W1's first line of trope.   **3.** In addition to the tripartite line division, there is significant use of internal rhyme in the second and third lines of troping: the use of *e* in "inviolate virginis alme nate paterque," and the use of *a* in "Sanguinis unda pectora munda perpetuamque."   **4.** The poet creates a parallelism here, linking the offspring and the Father.   **5.** This line is unusual in that it leads into the last line of the ordinary text, and thus does not make sense unless it is combined with those final words. A more idiomatic translation might incorporate the last line of the parent chant text, and would read "by the flow of your blood, cleanse our hearts, and give us eternal peace."

Facsimile

Herzog August Bibliothek Wolfenbüttel,
Cod. Guelf. 628 Helmst., Fascicle X

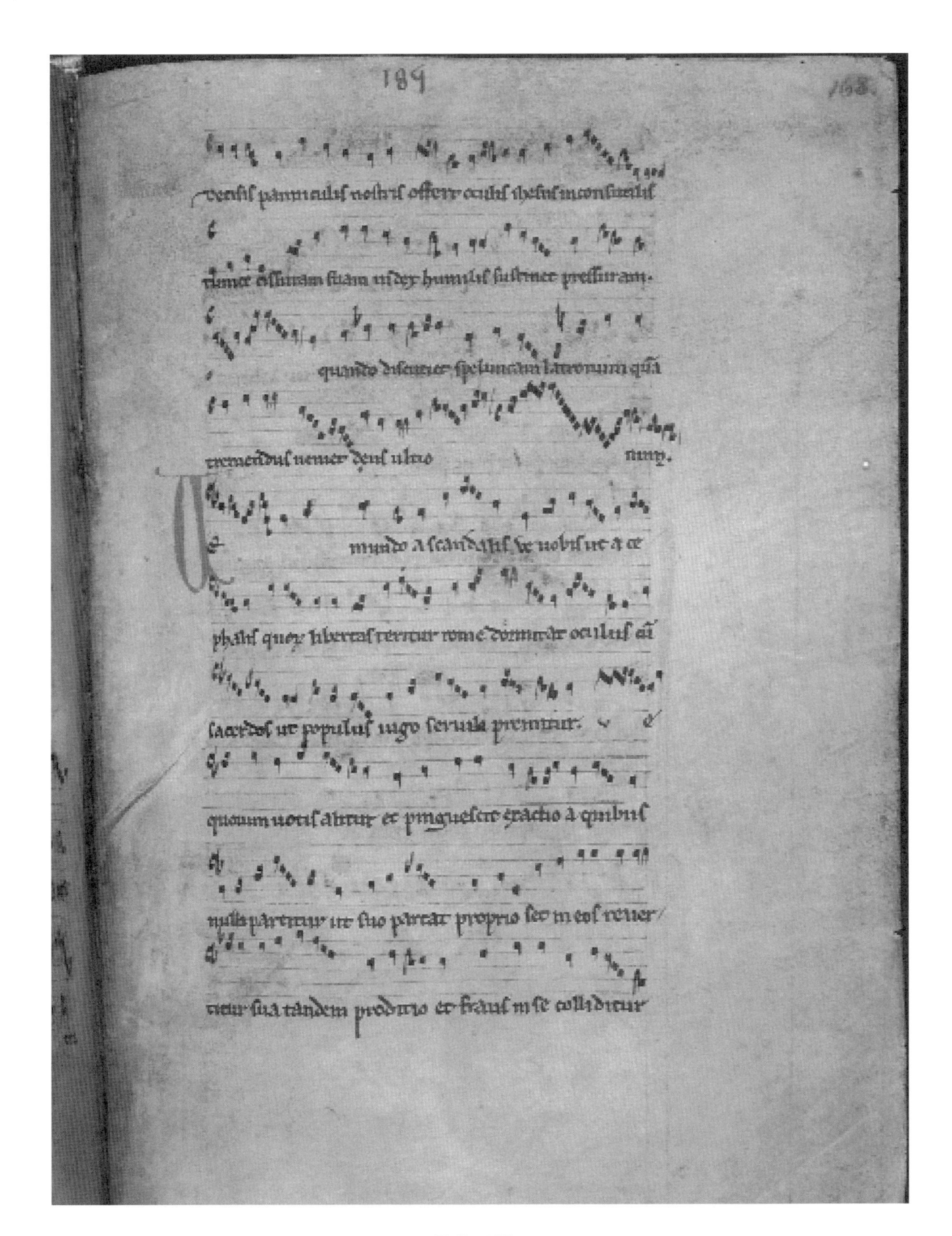

versis parmeulis nostris offert oculis ihesus inconsuetis

timet cissuram suam videy humilis sustinet pressuram.

quando discurrit speluncam latronum quia

tremendus venter deus ultro   nunc.

mundo a scandalis se nobis ut a ce-

phalis quore libertas teritur rome dormiret oculus cū

sacerdos ut populus iugo servili premitur.

quorum votis alitur et pinguescere exactio a quibus

nulla partitur ut suo parcat proprio seu in eos verte-

retur sua tandem proditio et fraus in se colliditur

iusto dei iudi... a o. Ha... Vnum

quo te uertere uinea qua retonder in fouea stillans

suos colonos cum pari merore sinat ut labores di-

ripiantur hinc pater hinc patro... nus.

In rama sonat gemitus plorante rachel anglie

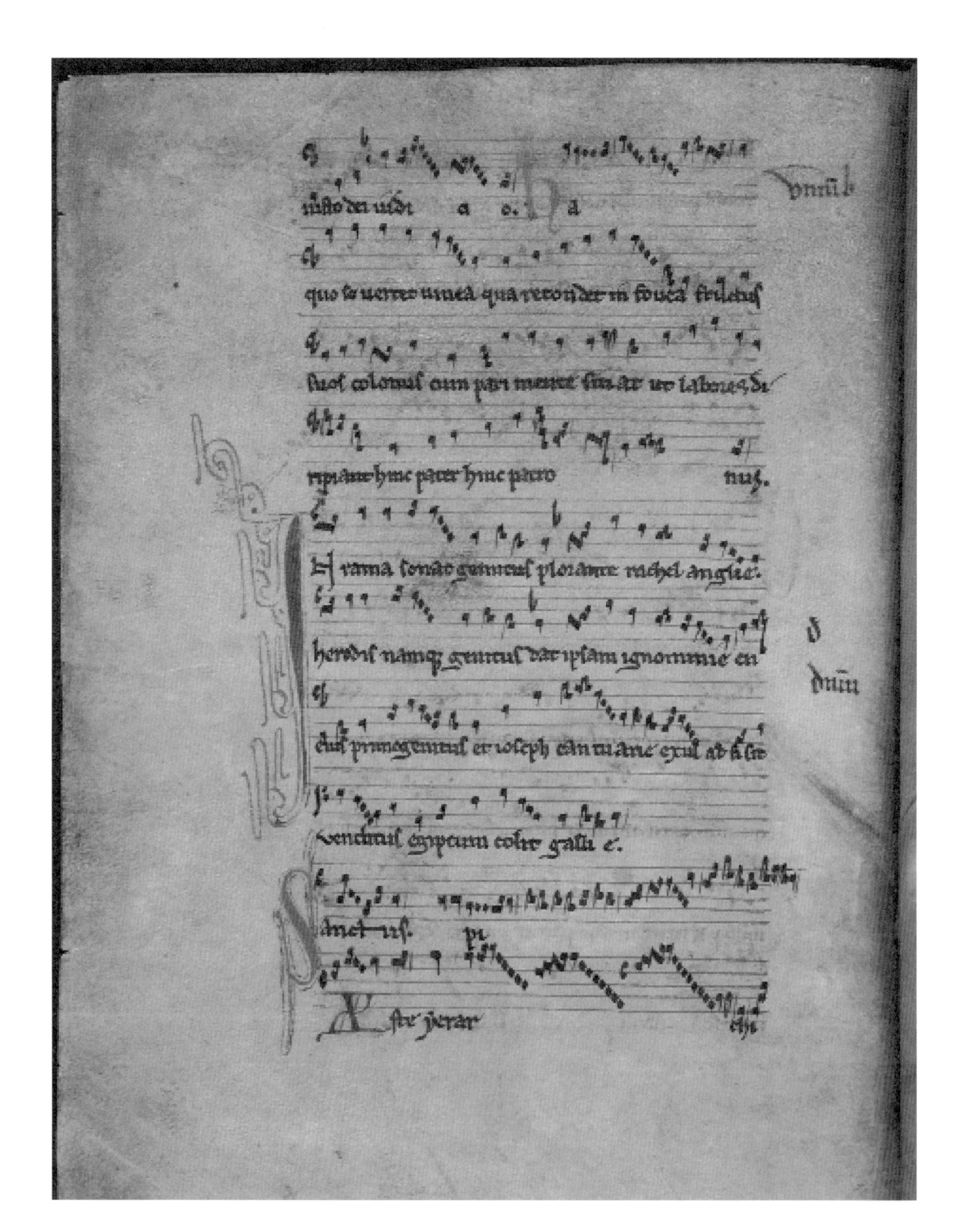

heredis namque gentius dat ipsam ignominie en-

dus primogenitus et ioseph cum maria exul ad fic-

...ceditur egyptum coste gallie.

...net us... pi

...ste ierar... chi...

Folio 185v

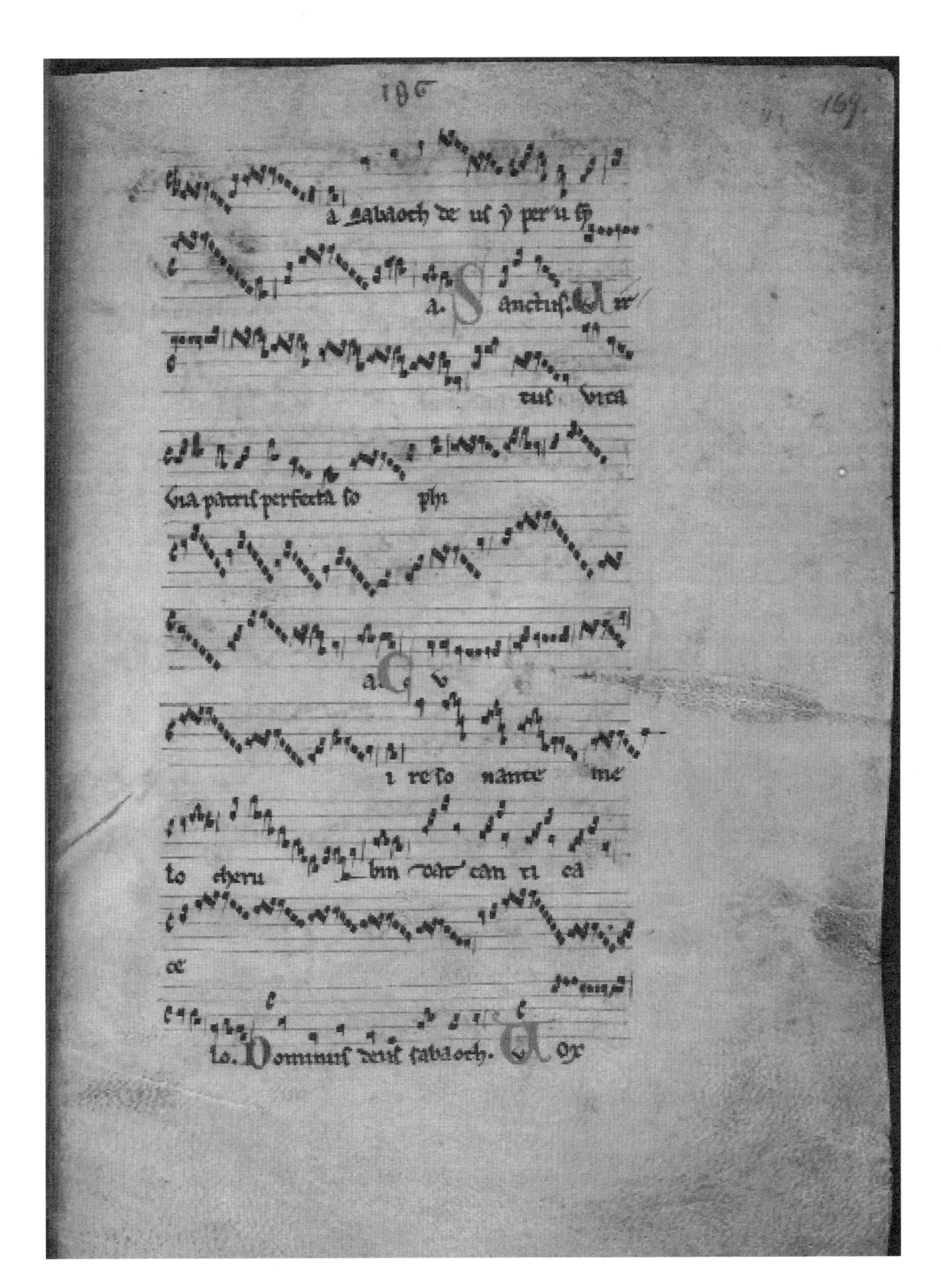

Folio 186r

quonium tota

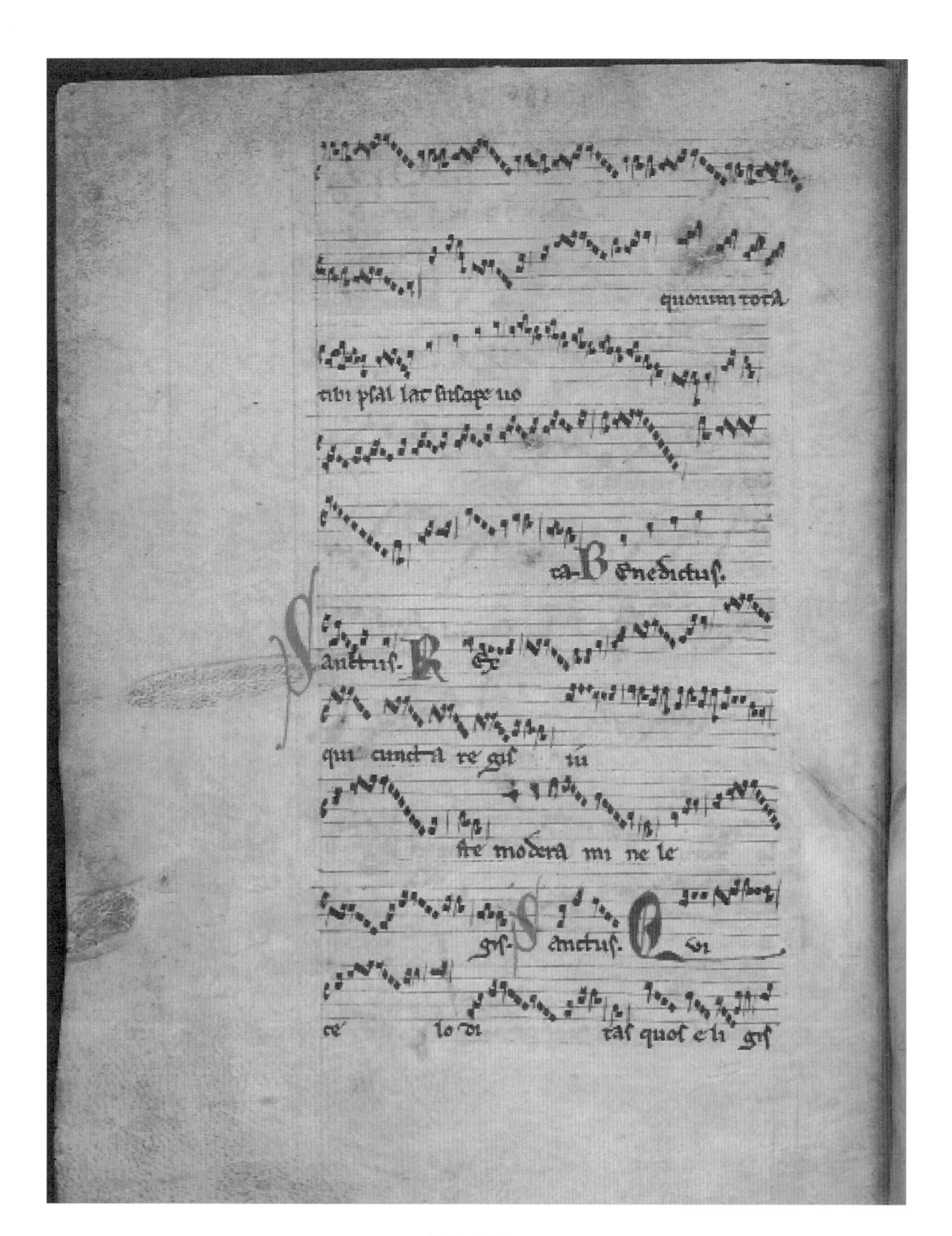

tibi psallat suscipe uo

ta Benedictus.

Sanctus Rex

qui cuncta regis tu

tre moderamine le

gis. Sanctus Qui

ce lo di tas quot eli gis

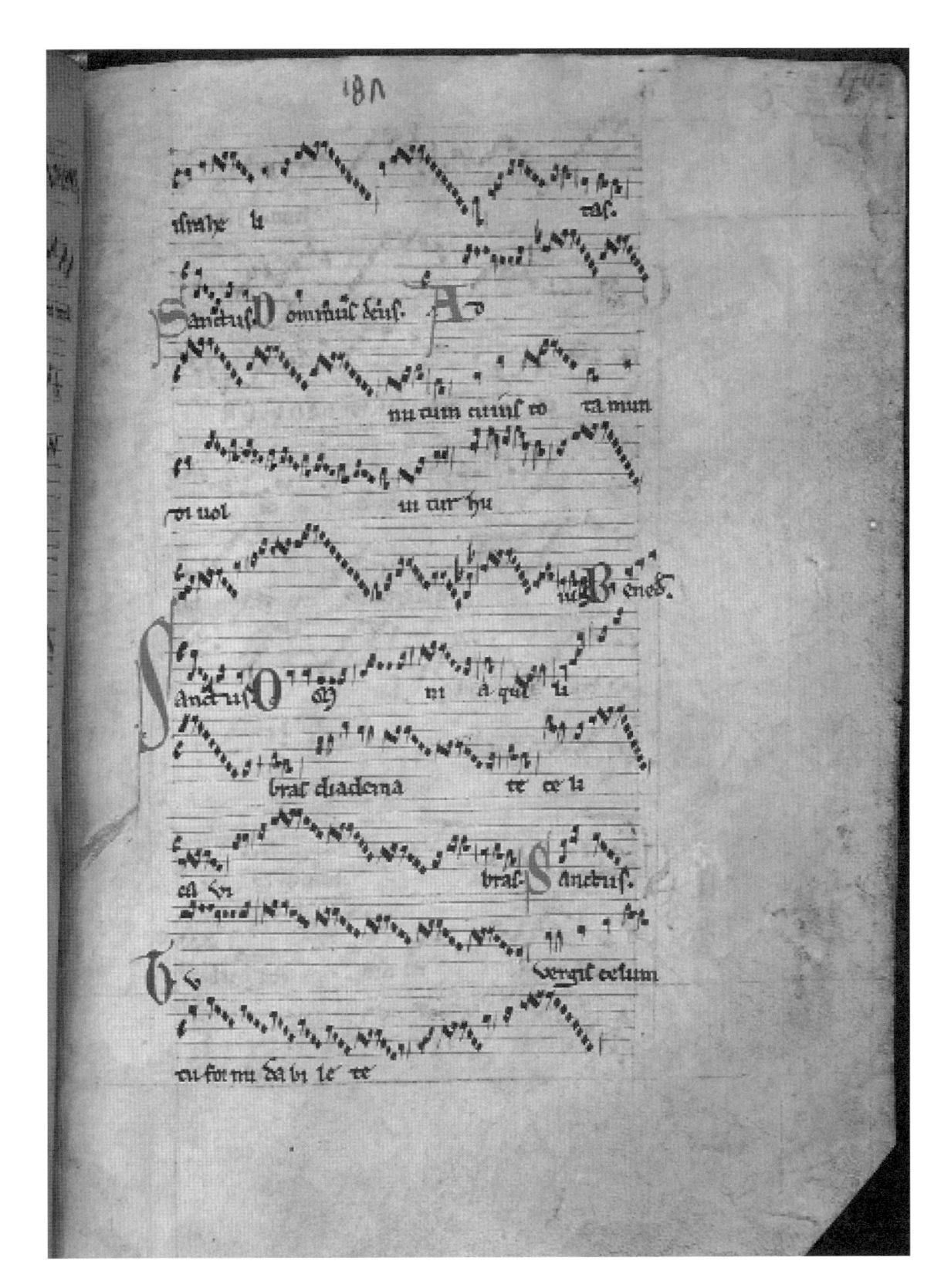

Folio 187r

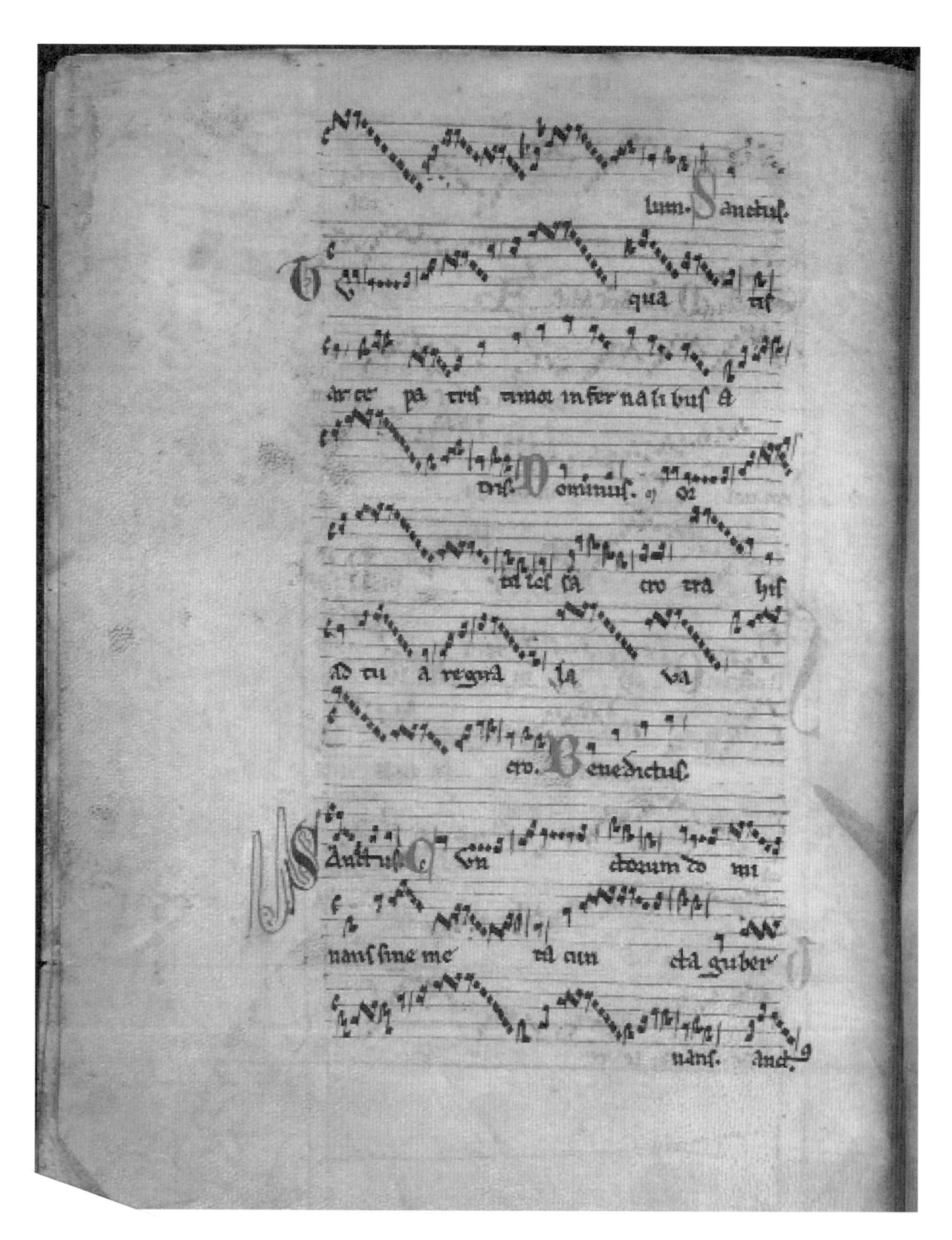

Folio 187v

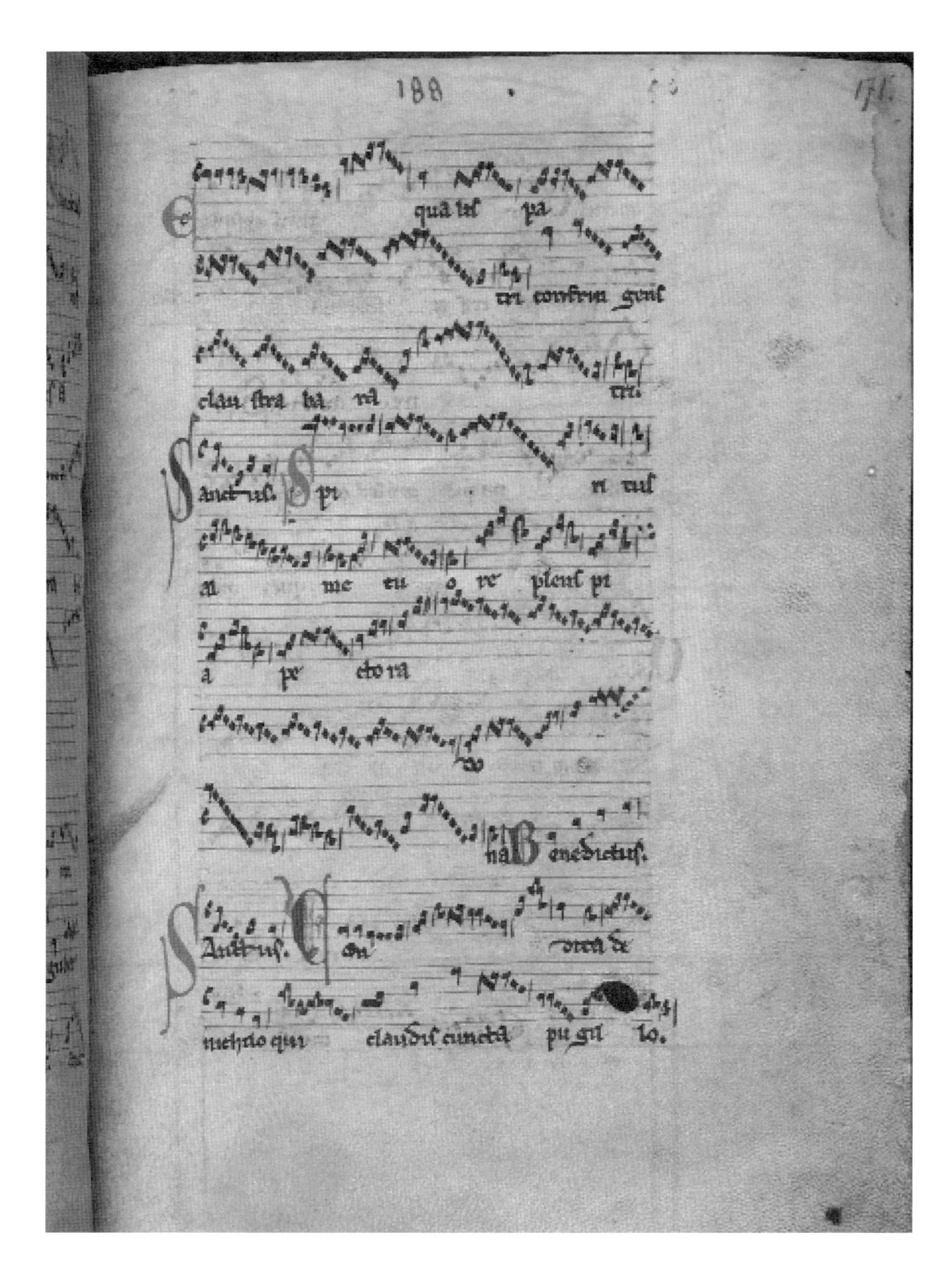

Folio 188r

anctus. Vir- ginis absque

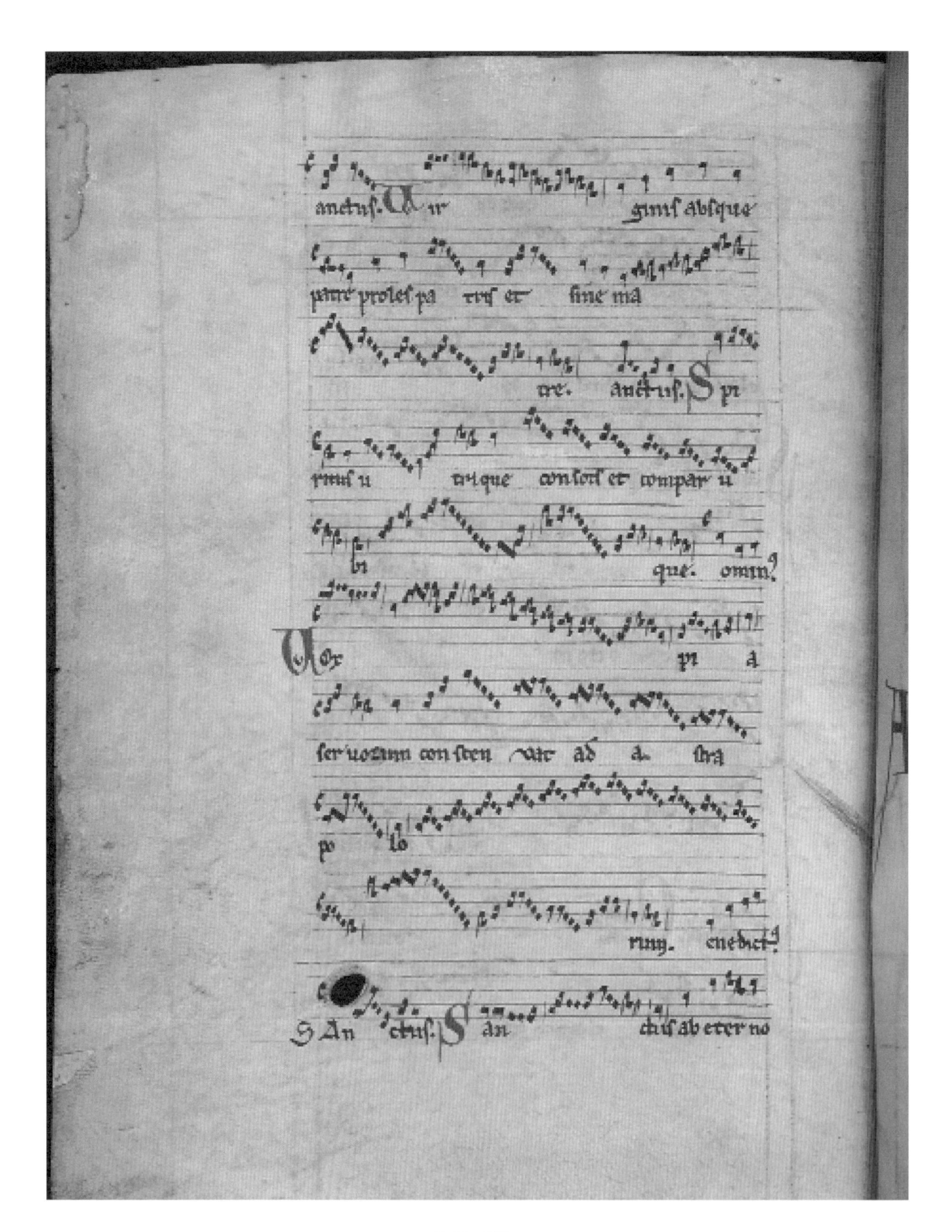

patre proles pa tris et sine ma

tre. anctus. Spi

ritus u trique consors et compar u

bi- que. omni-

Vox pi- a

servorum consten- uat ad a- stra

po- lo-

rum. enedic-

Sanctus. San- ctus ab eterno

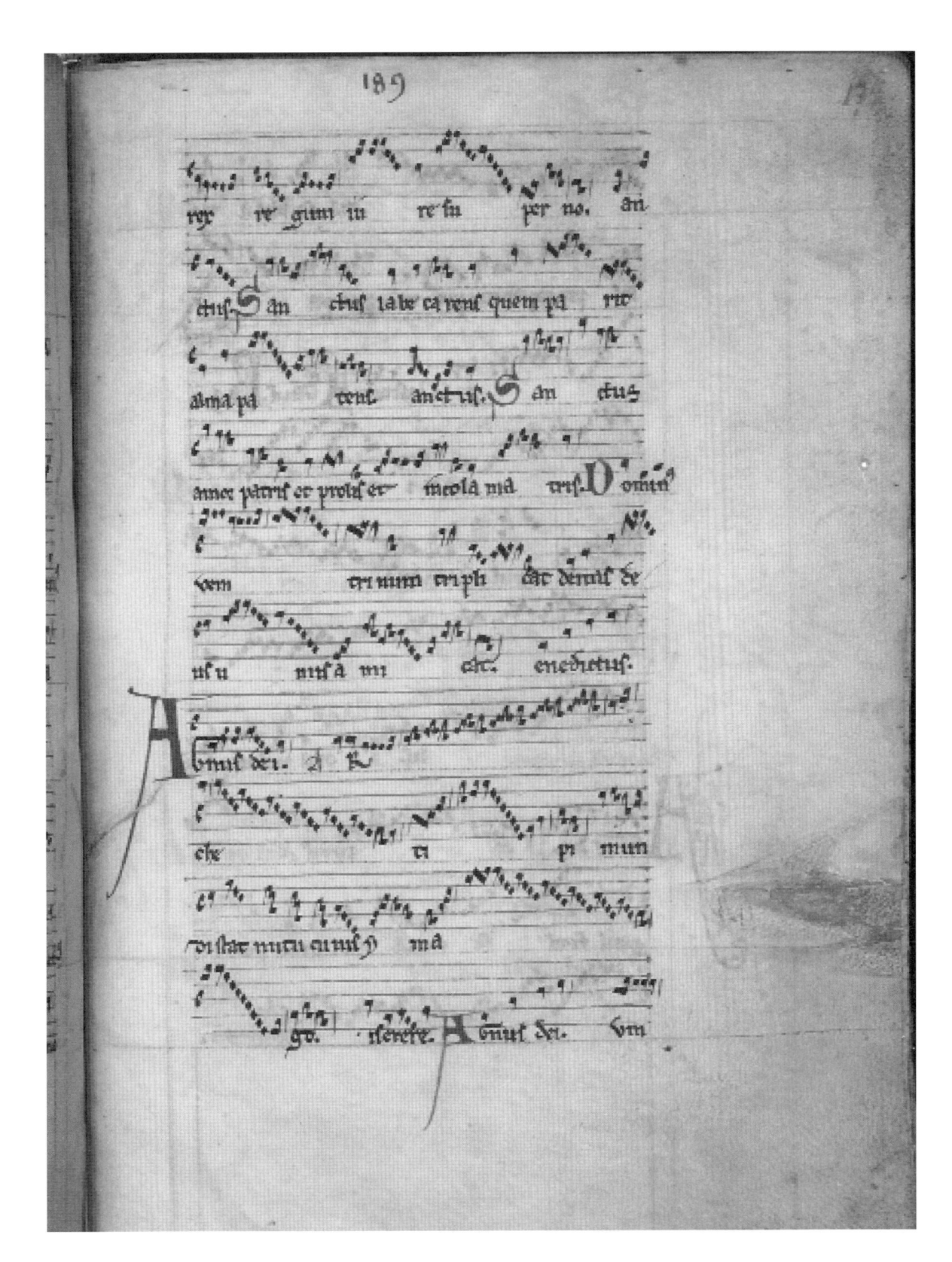

Folio 189r

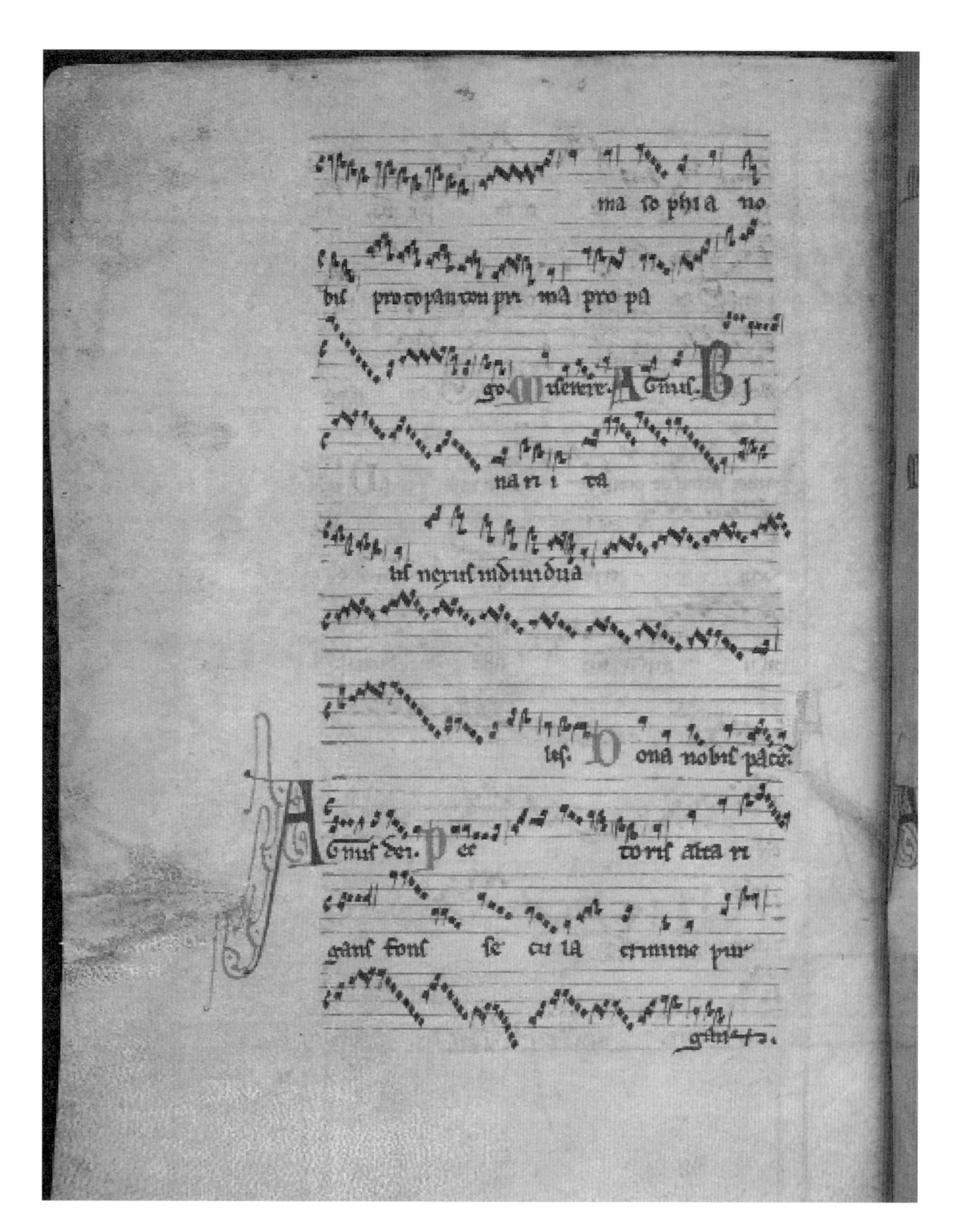

ma so phi a no
bis pro to pan ton pri ma pro pa
go miserere. Agnus. B
na ri ta
tis nexus individua
les. Dona nobis pacem.
Agnus dei. Peccatoris alta ri
gans fons secula crimine pur
gatus.

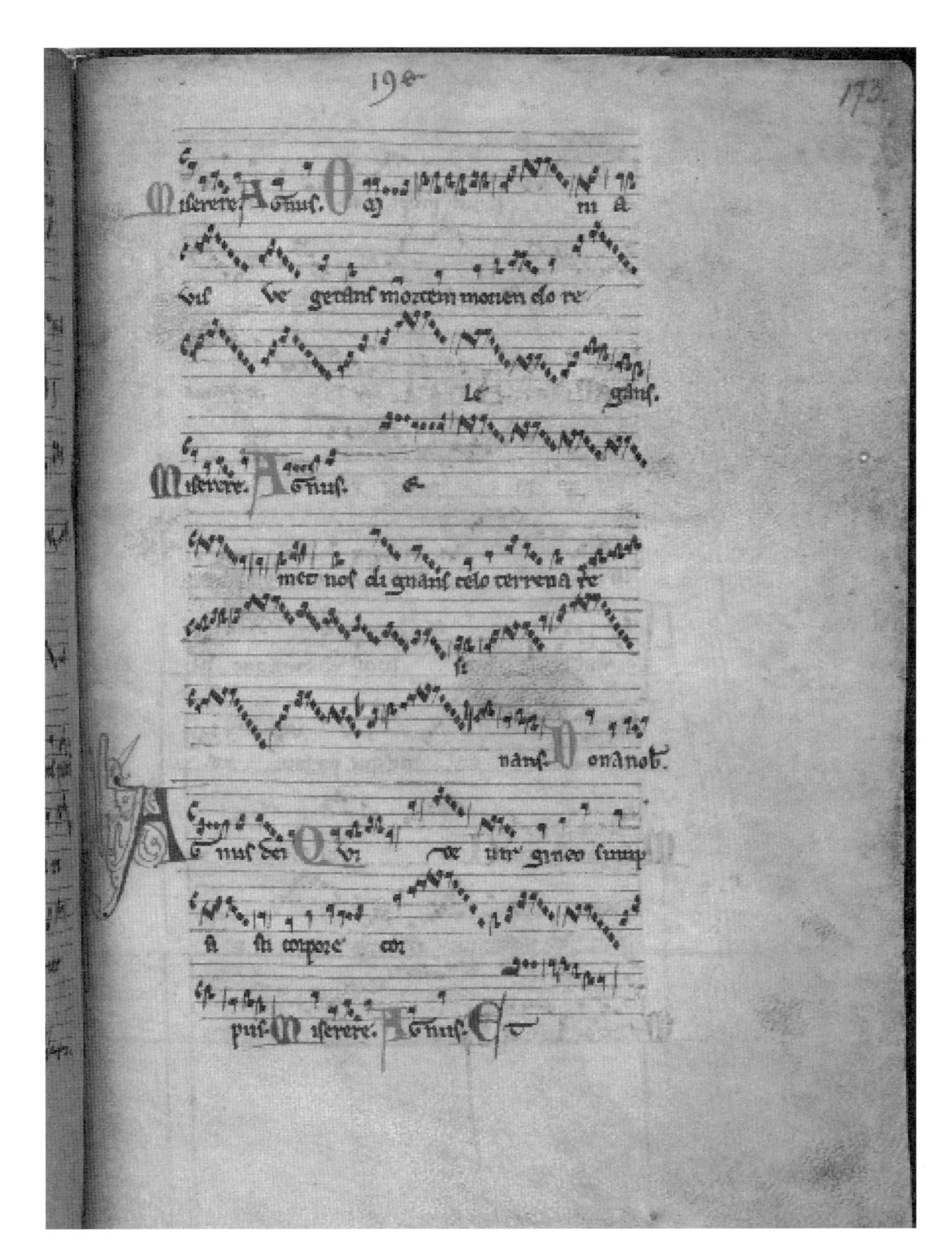

Folio 190r

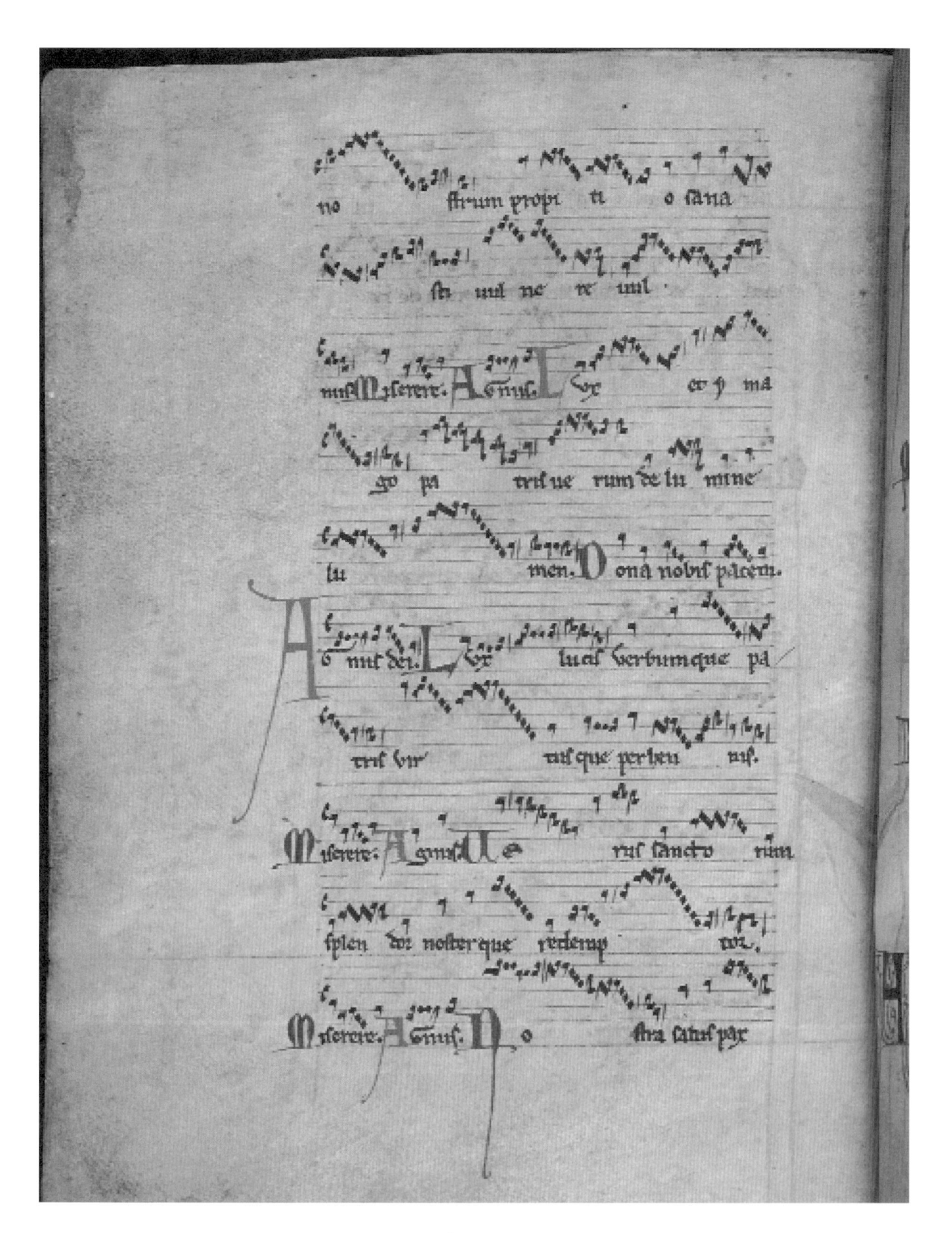

no strum propiti o sana
sti mul ne re imul
mus Miserere. Agnus. Lux et p ma
go pa tris ue rum de lu mine
lu men. Dona nobis pacem.

Agnus dei. Lux lucis verbumque pa
tris virtusque perhennis.
Miserere. Agnus De rus sancto rum
splen dor nosterque redemp tor.
Miserere. Agnus D o stra satis pax

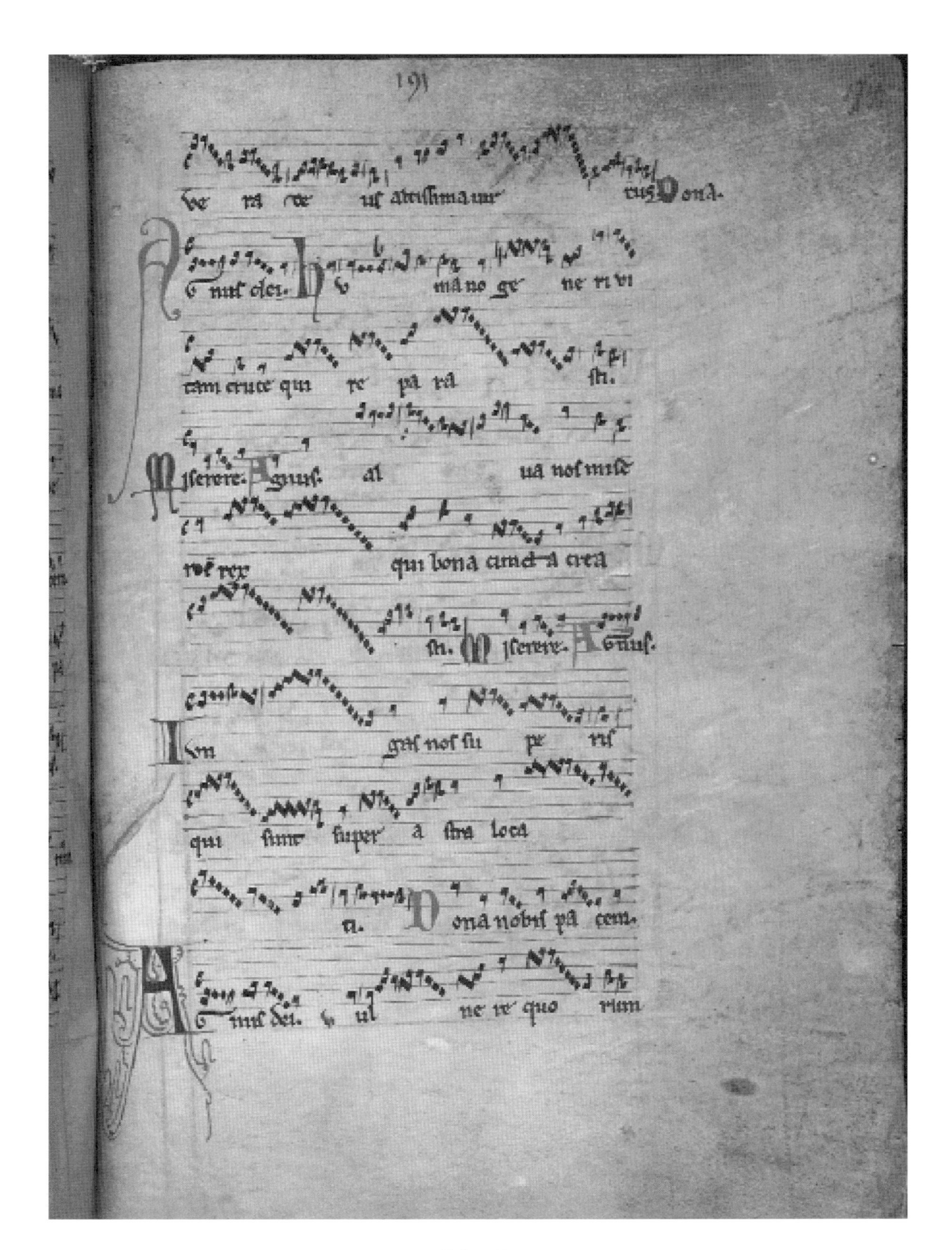

Folio 191r

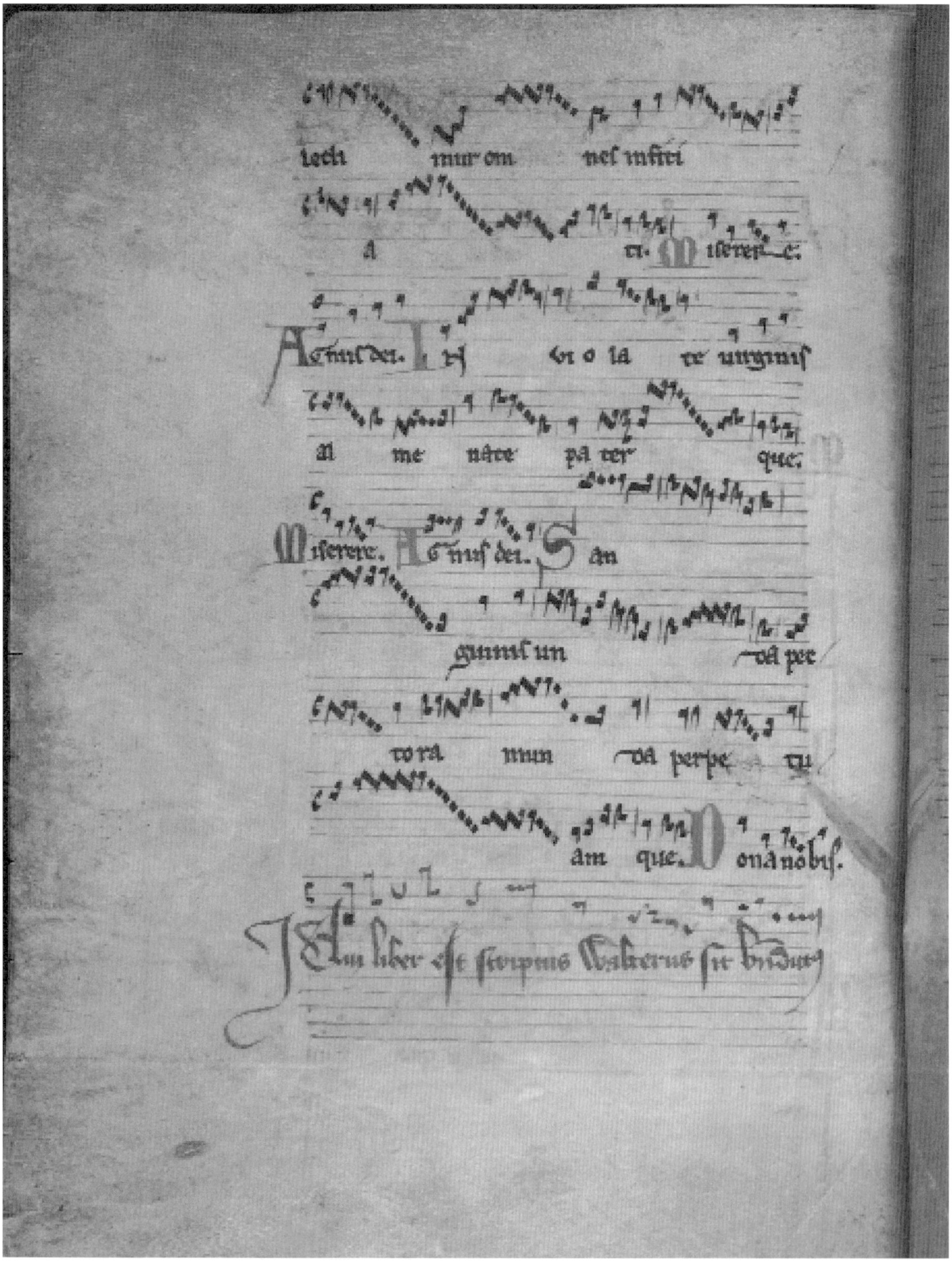

Folio 191v

Folio 192r

Folio 192v

Monophonic Tropes and Conductus of W1

Conductus

1. Quomodo cantabimus

fol. 185r

Quo--mo- do can- ta- bi- mus sub i- ni- qua le- ge.

O- ves quid at- ten- di- mus. Lu- pus est in gre- ge.

De- ci- sis pan- ni- cu- lis no- stris of- fert o- cu- lis

Ihe- sus in con- su- ti- lis tu- ni- ce cis- su- ram

su- am iu- dex hu- mi- lis su- sti- net pres- su- ram.

O quan- do di- scu- ti- et spe- lun- cam la- tro- num

quam tre- men- dus ve- ni- et de- us ul- ti- o-

-num.

2. Ve mundo a scandalis

fols. 185r–185v

Ve mundo a scandalis ve vobis ut acephalis quorum libertas teritur rome dormitat oculus cum sacerdos ut populus iugo servili premitur. Ve quorum votis alitur et pinquescit exactio a quibus nulli parcitur ut suo parcant proprio set in eos revertitur sua tandem proditio et fraus in se colliditur iusto dei iudicio.

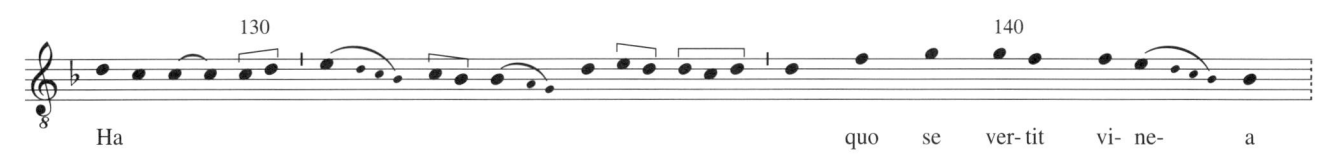

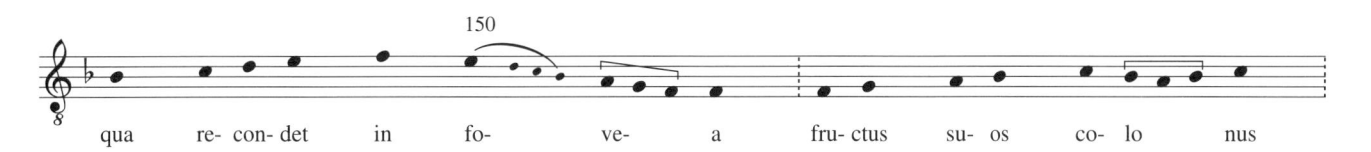

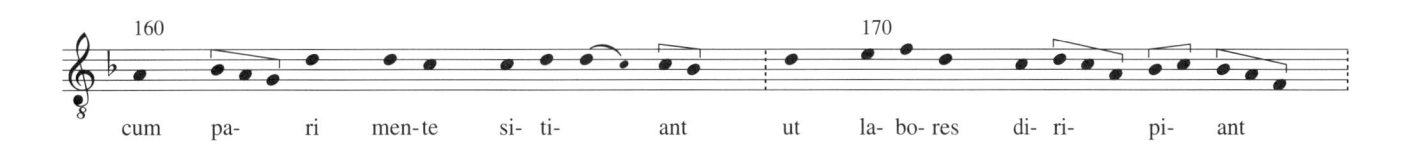

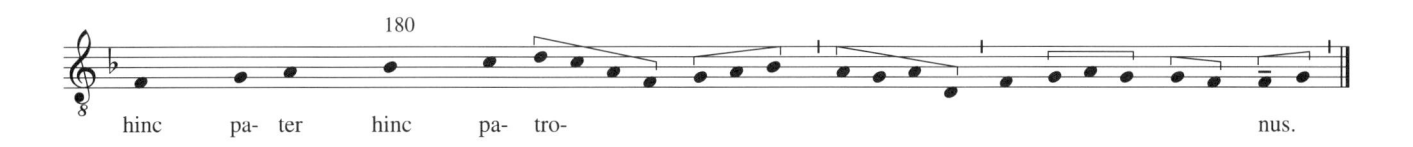

Ha ... quo se vertit vinea qua recondet in fovea fructus suos colonus cum pari mente sitiant ut labores diripiant hinc pater hinc patronus.

3. In Rama sonat gemitus

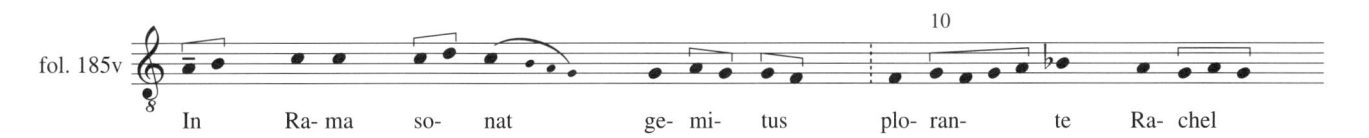

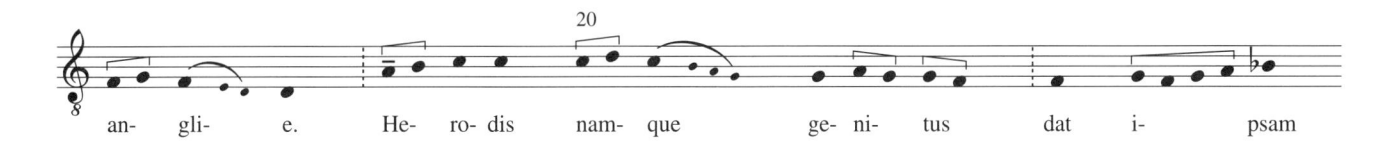

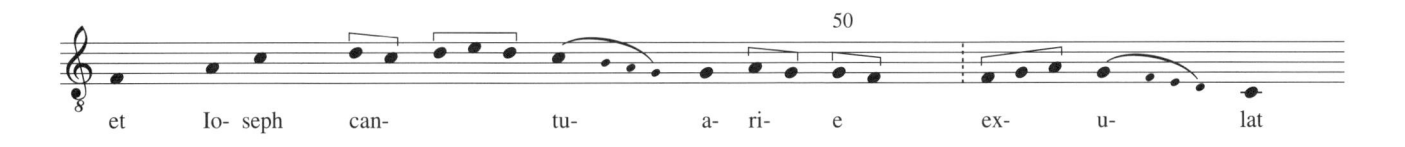

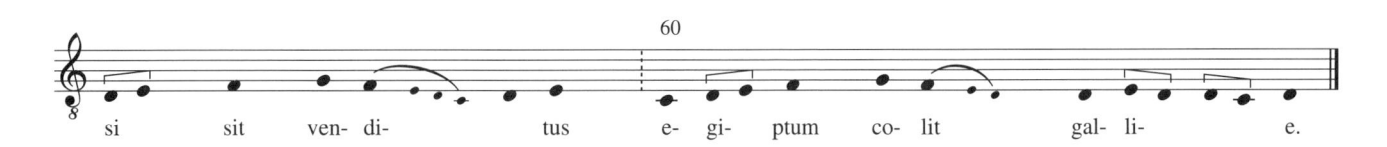

fol. 185v

In Rama sonat gemitus plorante Rachel anglie. Herodis namque genitus dat ipsam ignominie en eius primogenitus et Ioseph cantu arie exulat si sit venditus egiptum colit gallie.

Sanctus Tropes
4. Sanctus Christe yerarchia

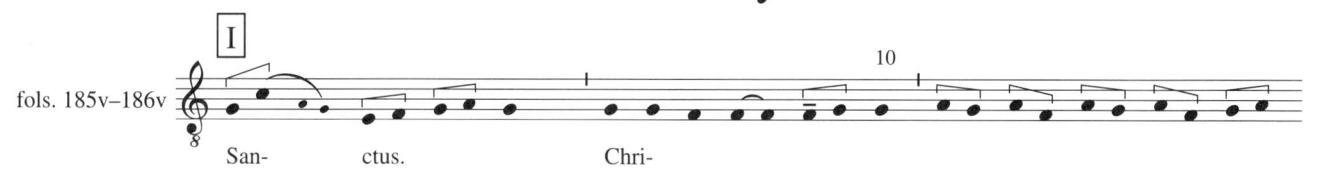

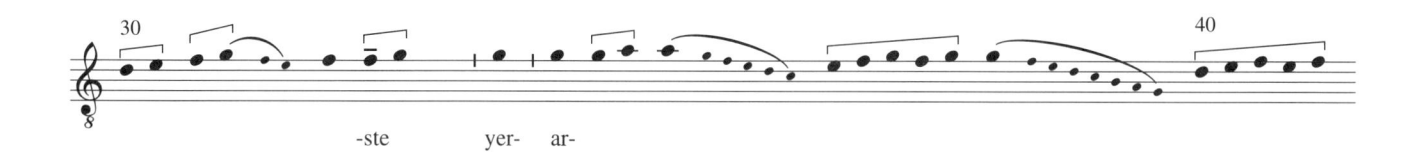

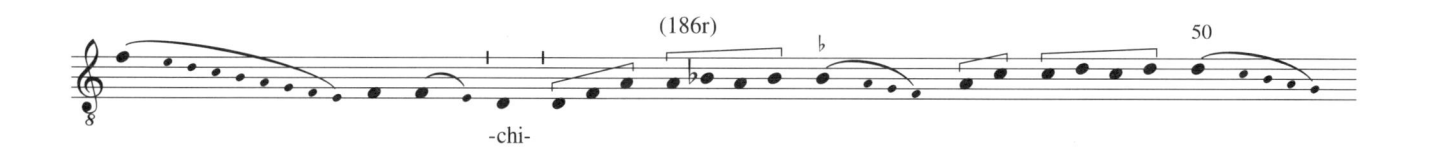

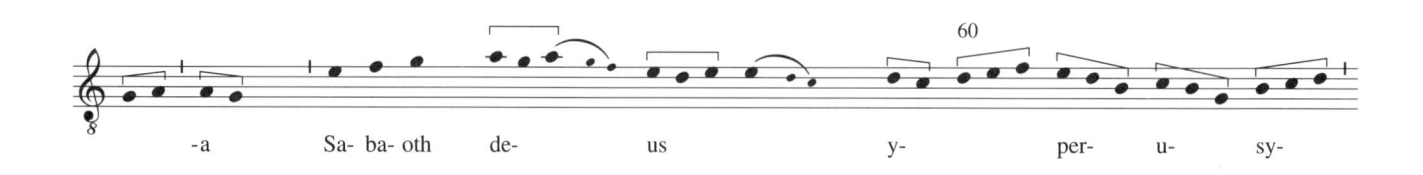

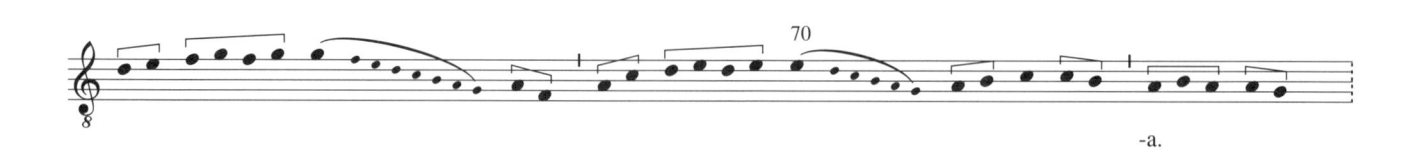

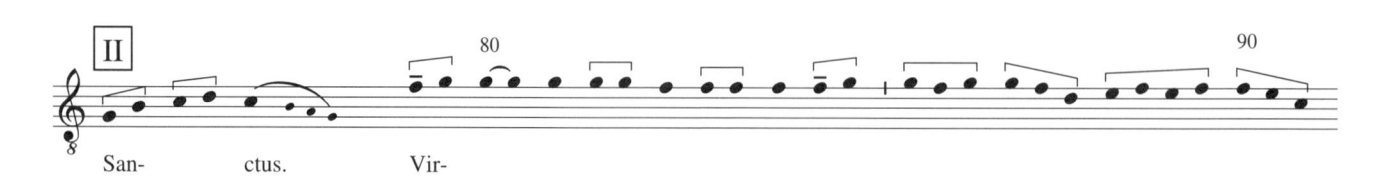

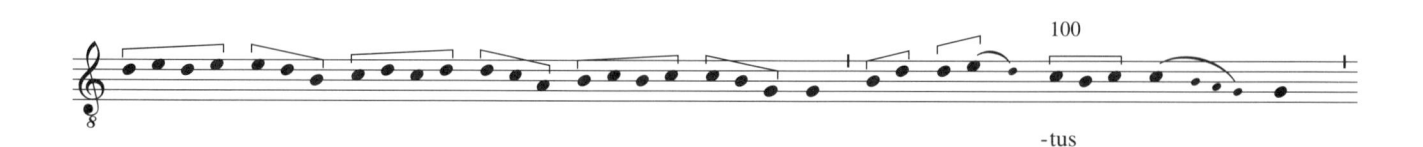

I

fols. 185v–186v

San- ctus. Chri-

-ste yer- ar-

-chi-

-a Sa- ba- oth de- us y- per- u- sy-

-a.

II

San- ctus. Vir-

-tus

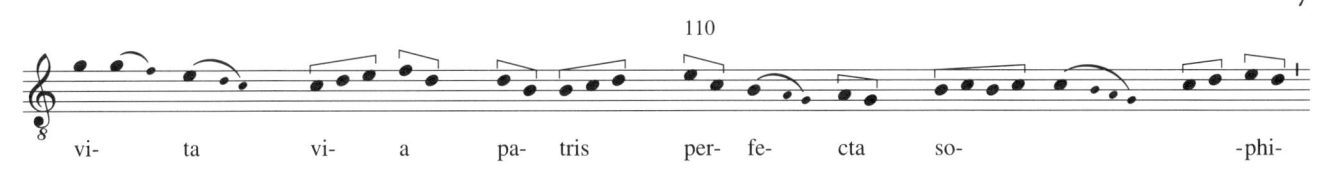

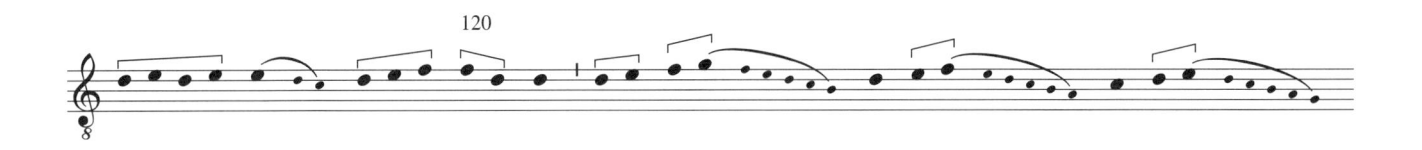

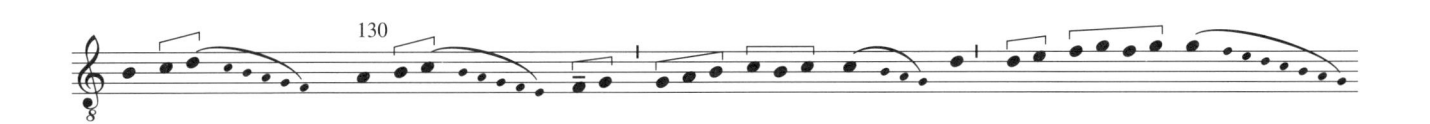

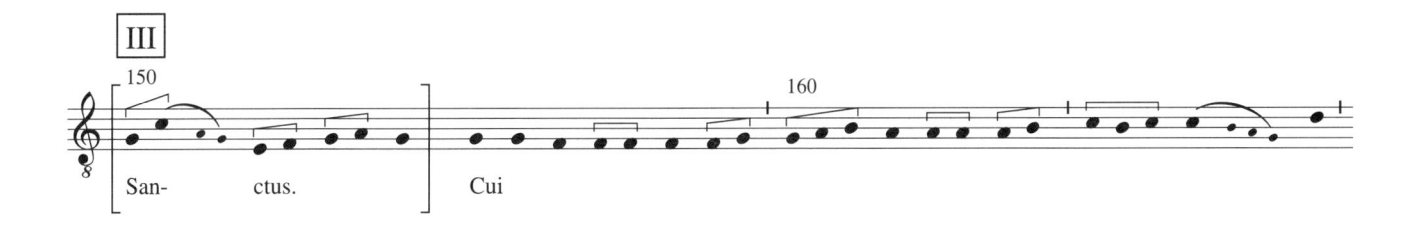

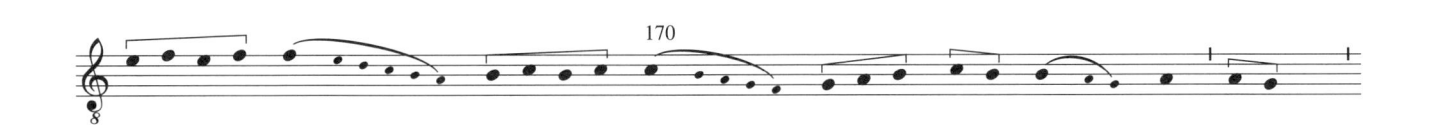

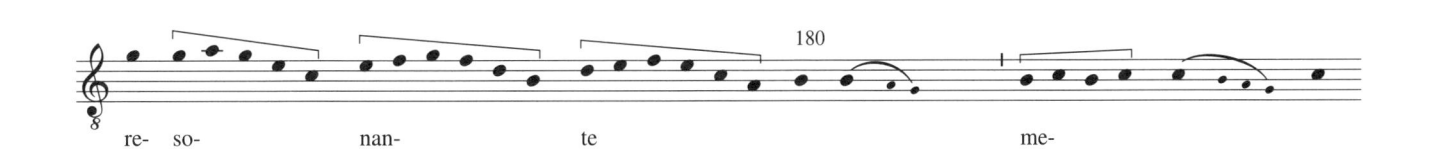

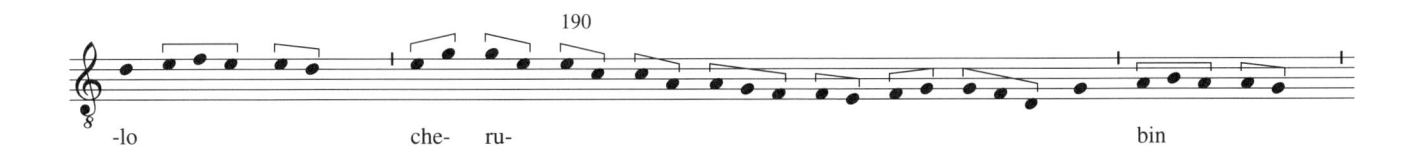

vi- ta vi- a pa- tris per- fe- cta so- -phi-

-a.

III

San- ctus. Cui

re- so- nan- te me-

-lo che- ru- bin

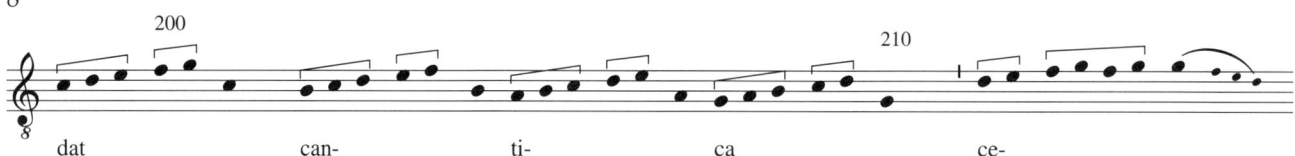

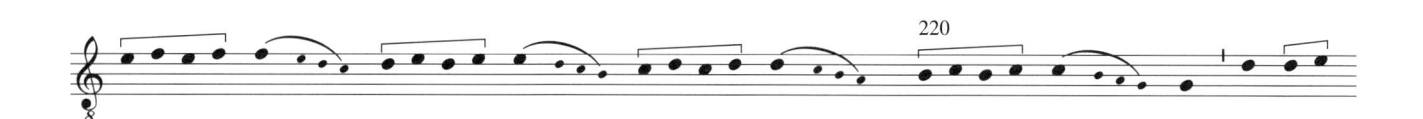

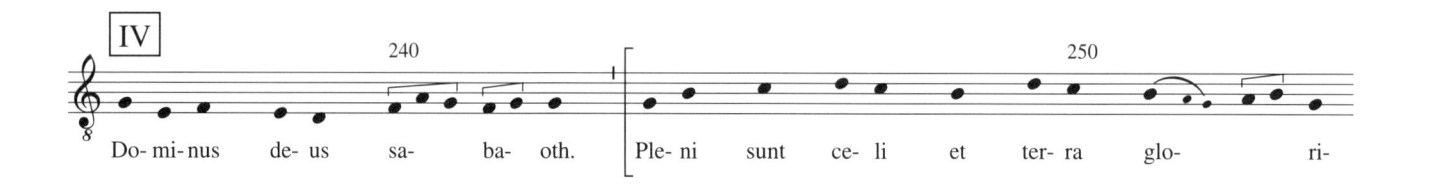

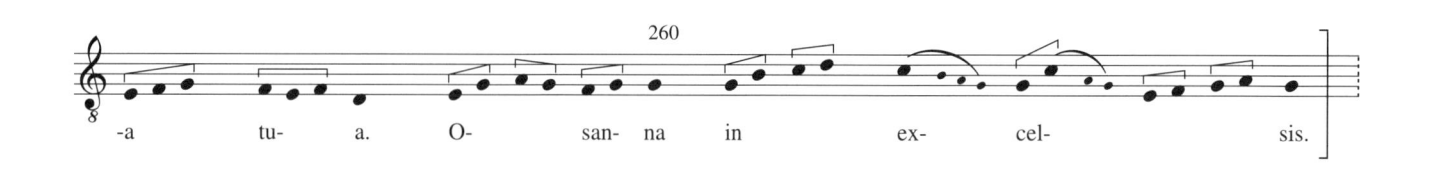

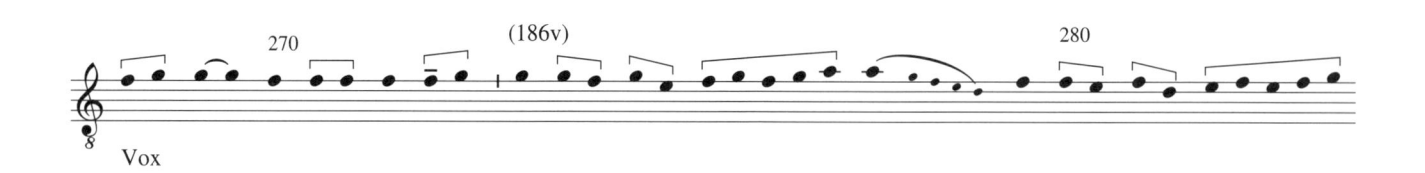

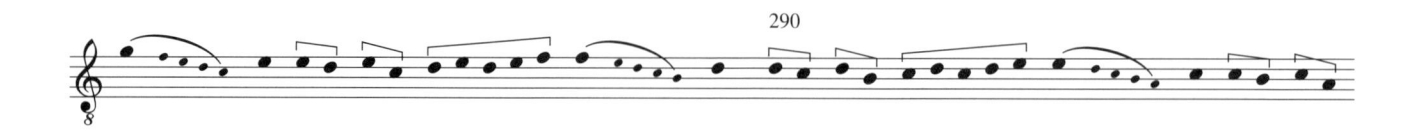

dat can- ti- ca ce-

-lo.

IV

Do- mi- nus de- us sa- ba- oth. Ple- ni sunt ce- li et ter- ra glo- ri-

-a tu- a. O- san- na in ex- cel- sis.

Vox

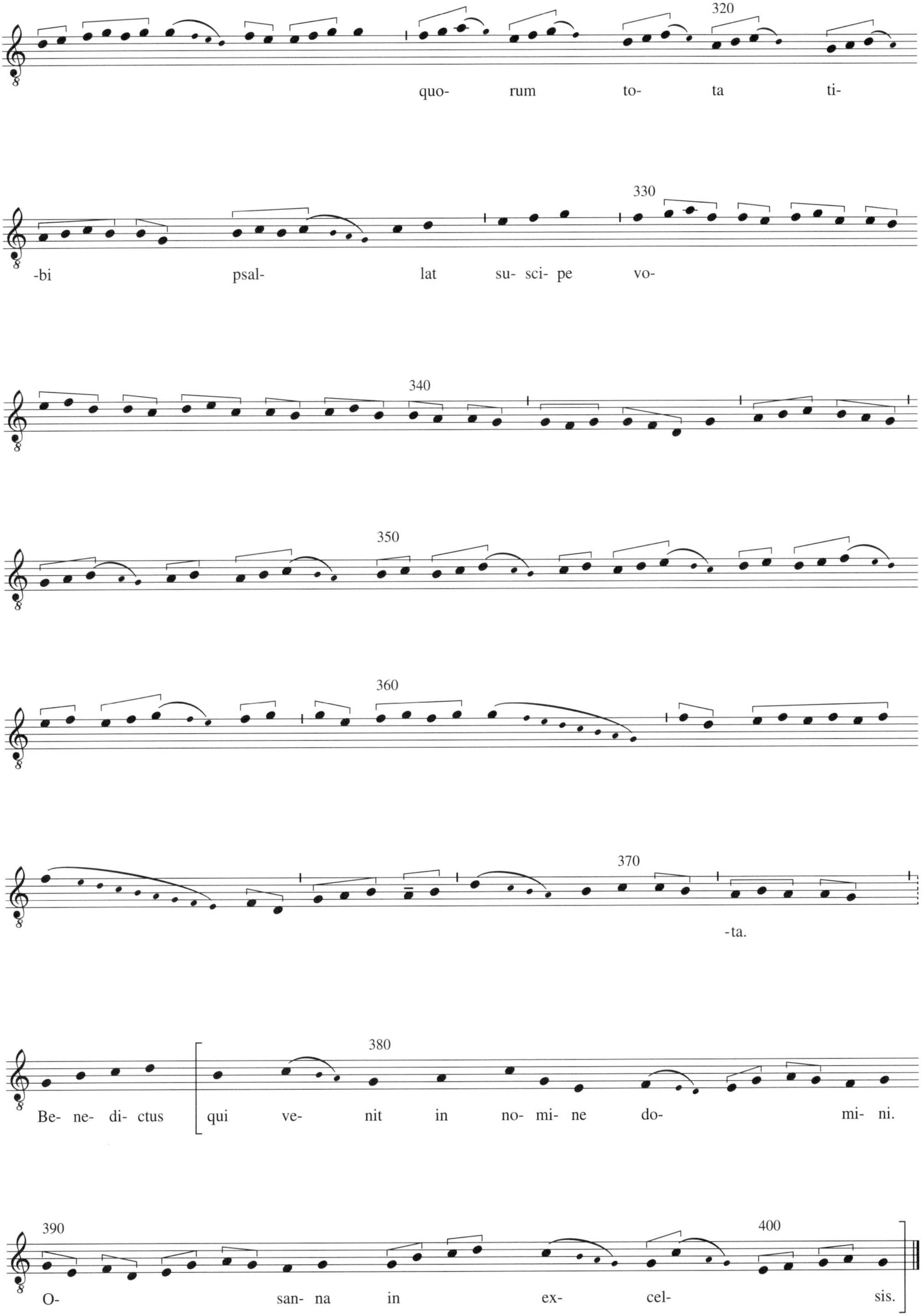
320
quo- rum to- ta ti-
330
-bi psal- lat su- sci- pe vo-
340
350
360
370
-ta.
380
Be- ne- di- ctus qui ve- nit in no- mi- ne do- mi- ni.
390
400
O- san- na in ex- cel- sis.

5. Sanctus Rex qui cuncta regis

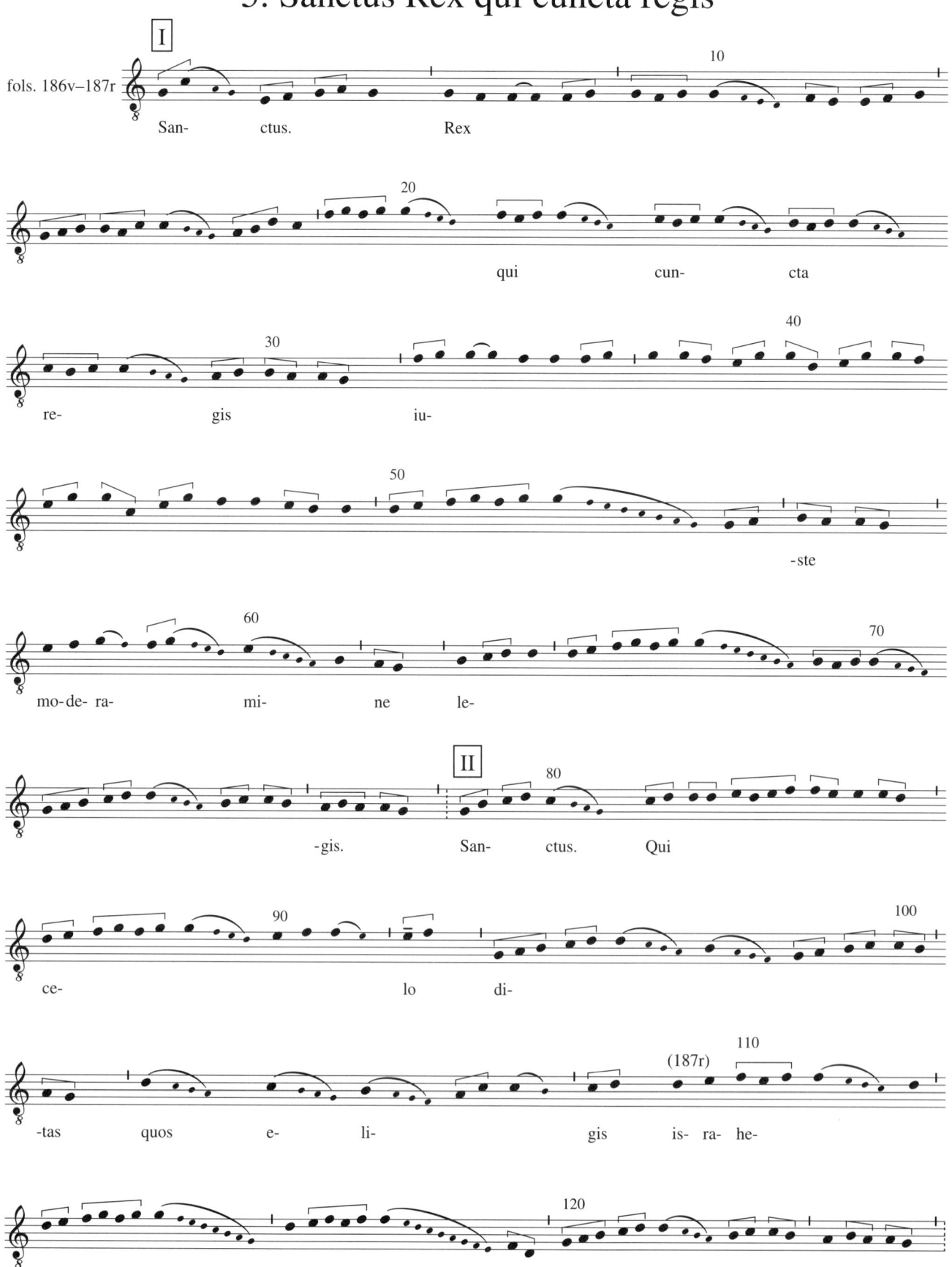

fols. 186v–187r

San- ctus. Rex qui cun- cta re- gis iu- -ste mo- de- ra- mi- ne le- -gis. San- ctus. Qui ce- lo di- -tas quos e- li- gis is- ra- he- -li- tas.

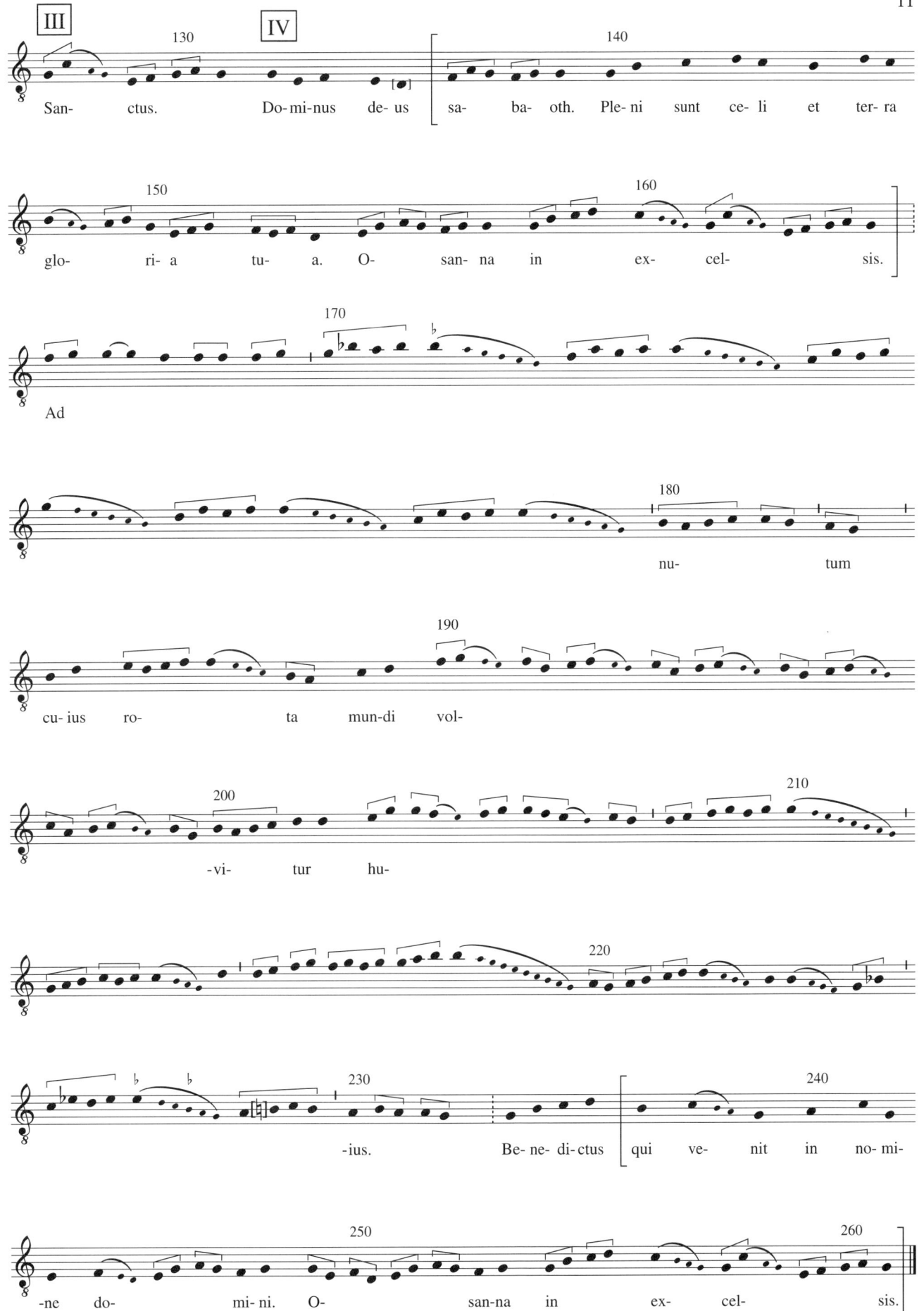

III San- ctus. Do-mi-nus de- us **IV** sa- ba- oth. Ple- ni sunt ce- li et ter- ra glo- ri- a tu- a. O- san- na in ex- cel- sis.

Ad nu- tum cu- ius ro- ta mun-di vol- -vi- tur hu- -ius. Be- ne- di-ctus qui ve- nit in no- mi- -ne do- mi- ni. O- san-na in ex- cel- sis.

6. Sanctus Omnia qui libras

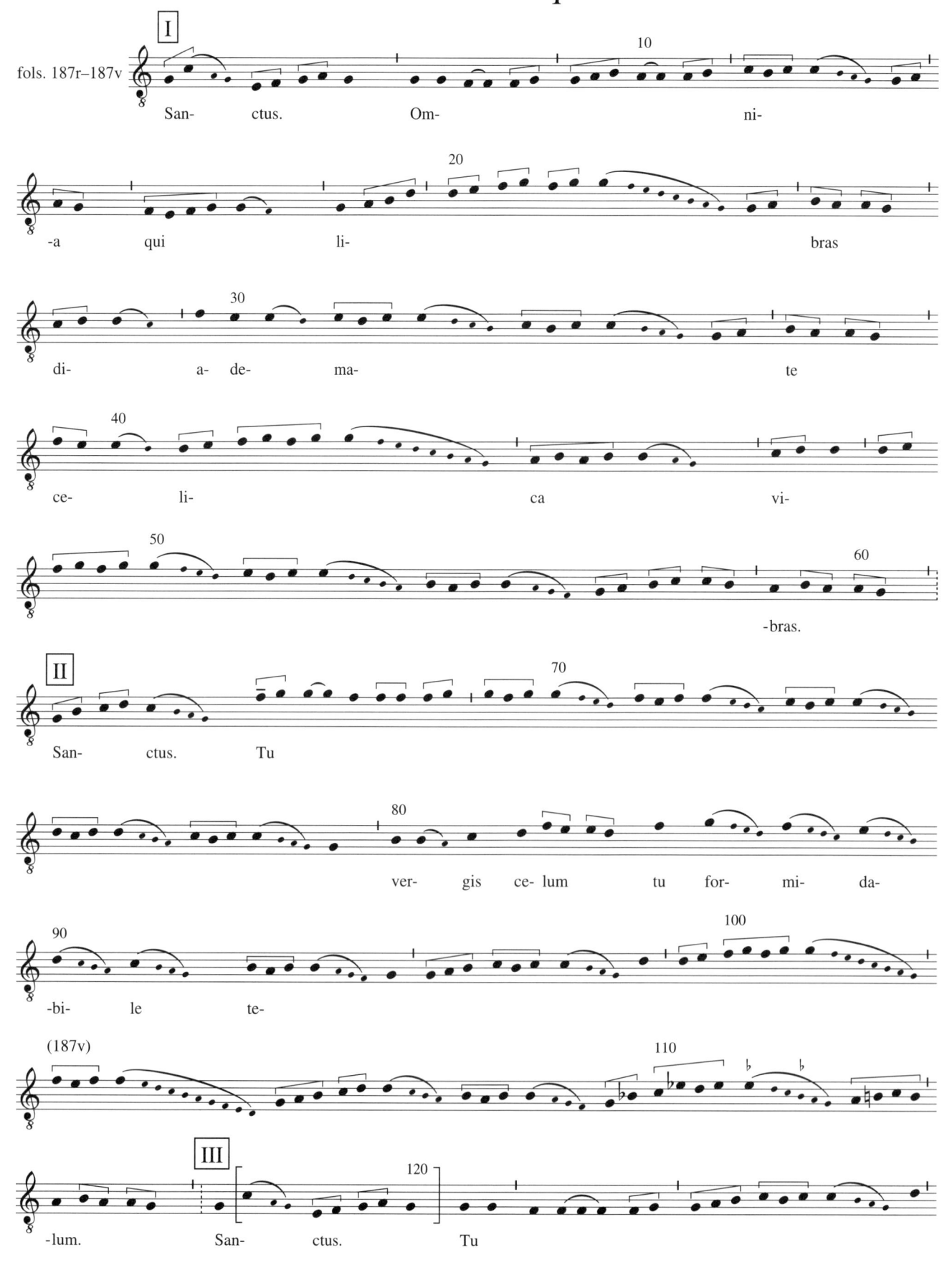

fols. 187r–187v

San- ctus. Om- ni- -a qui li- bras

di- a- de- ma- te

ce- li- ca vi- -bras.

San- ctus. Tu ver- gis ce- lum tu for- mi- da- -bi- le te-

(187v)

-lum. San- ctus. Tu

13

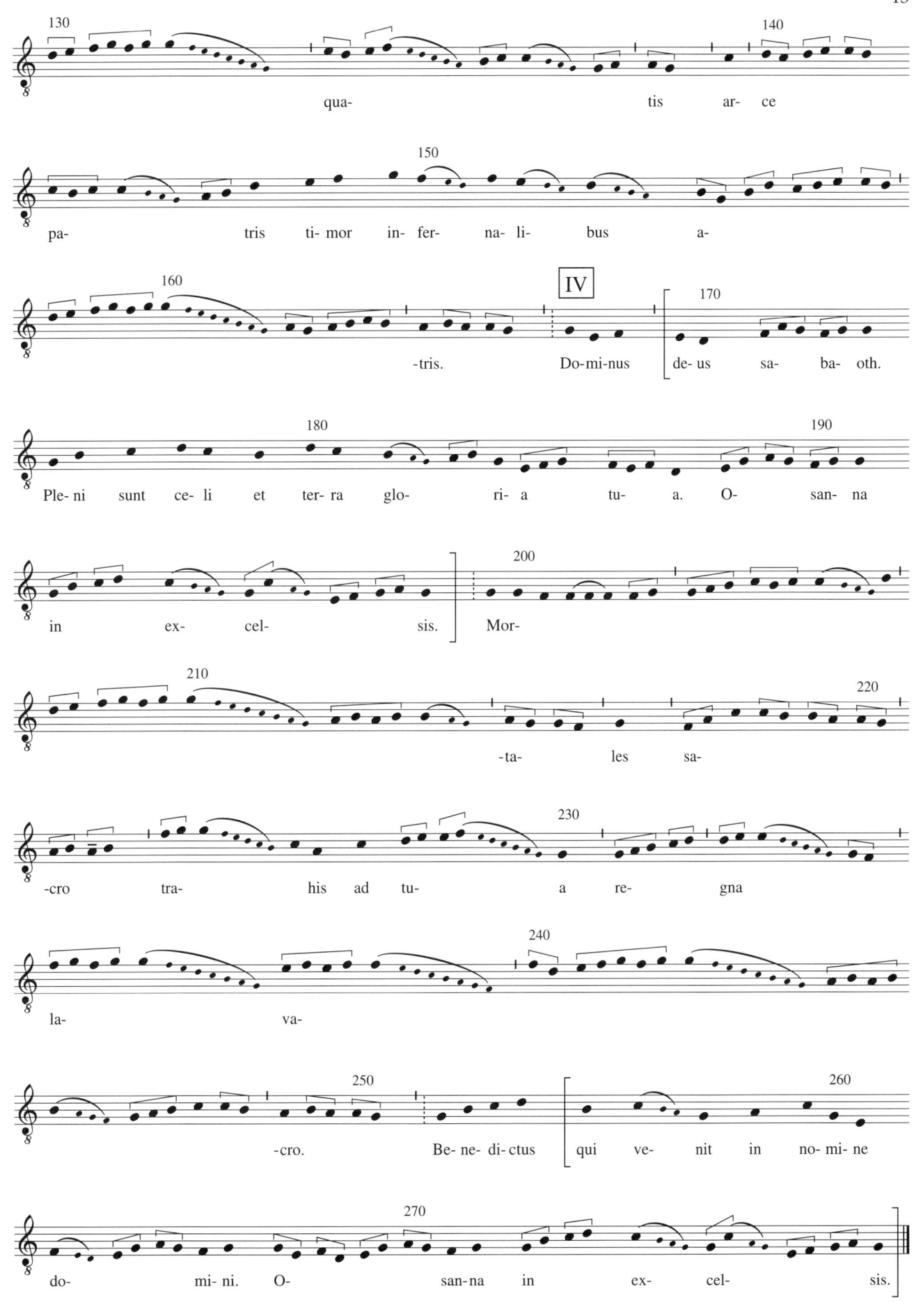

7. Sanctus Cunctorum dominans

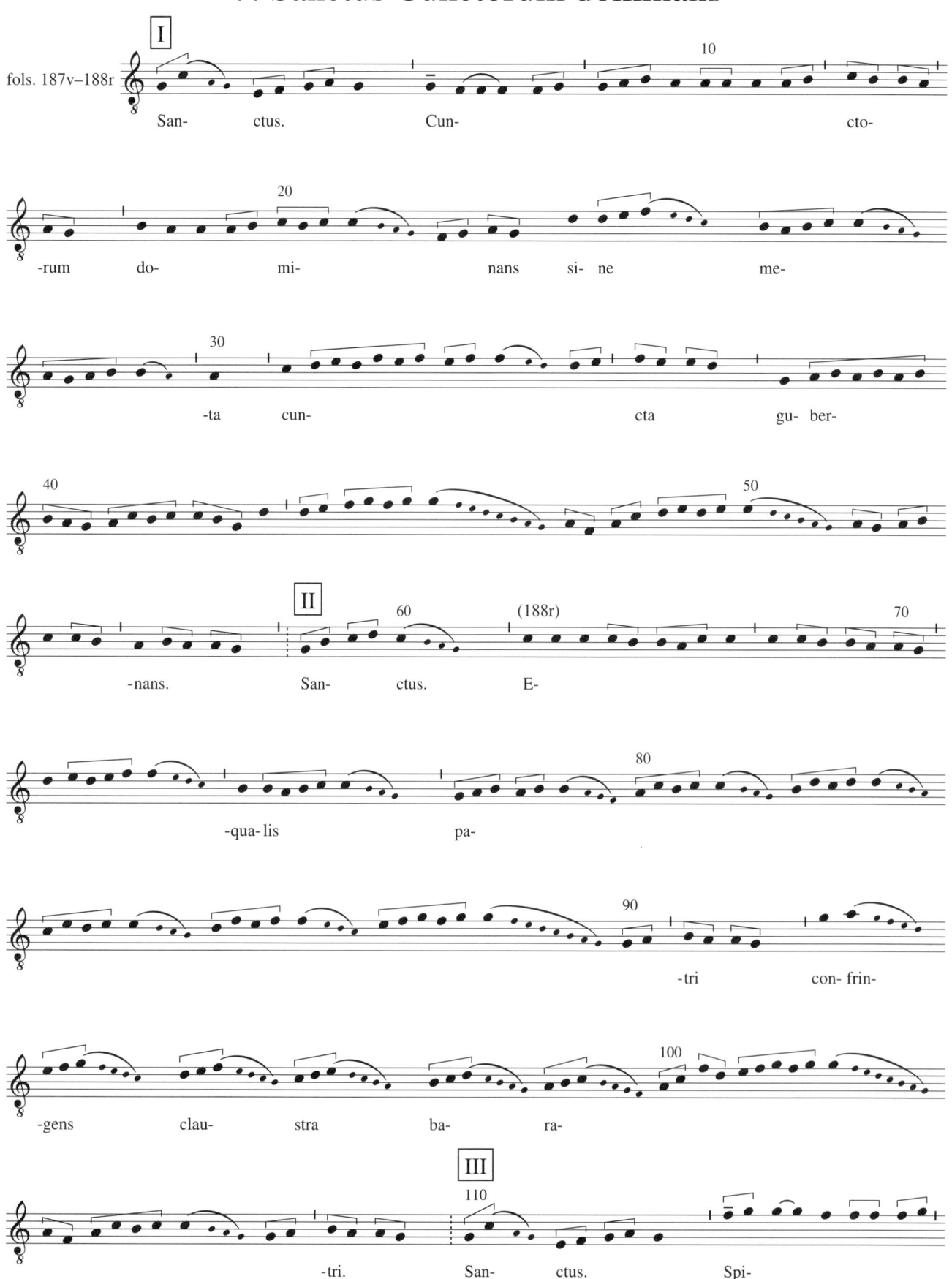

fols. 187v–188r

San- ctus. Cun- cto-

-rum do- mi- nans si- ne me-

-ta cun- cta gu- ber-

-nans. Sanctus. E-

-qua- lis pa-

-tri con- frin-

-gens clau- stra ba- ra-

-tri. San- ctus. Spi-

15

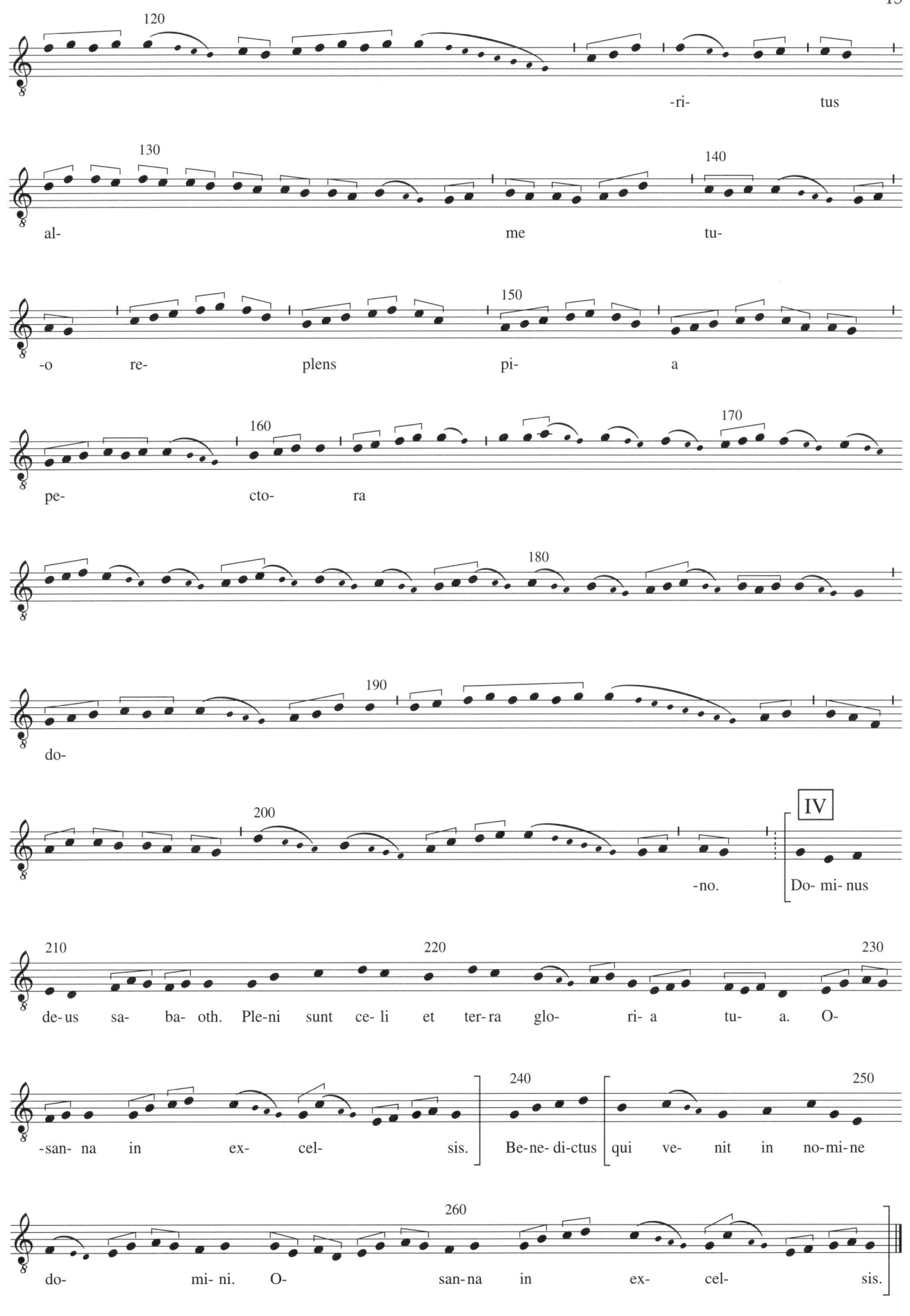

8. Sanctus Condita de nichilo

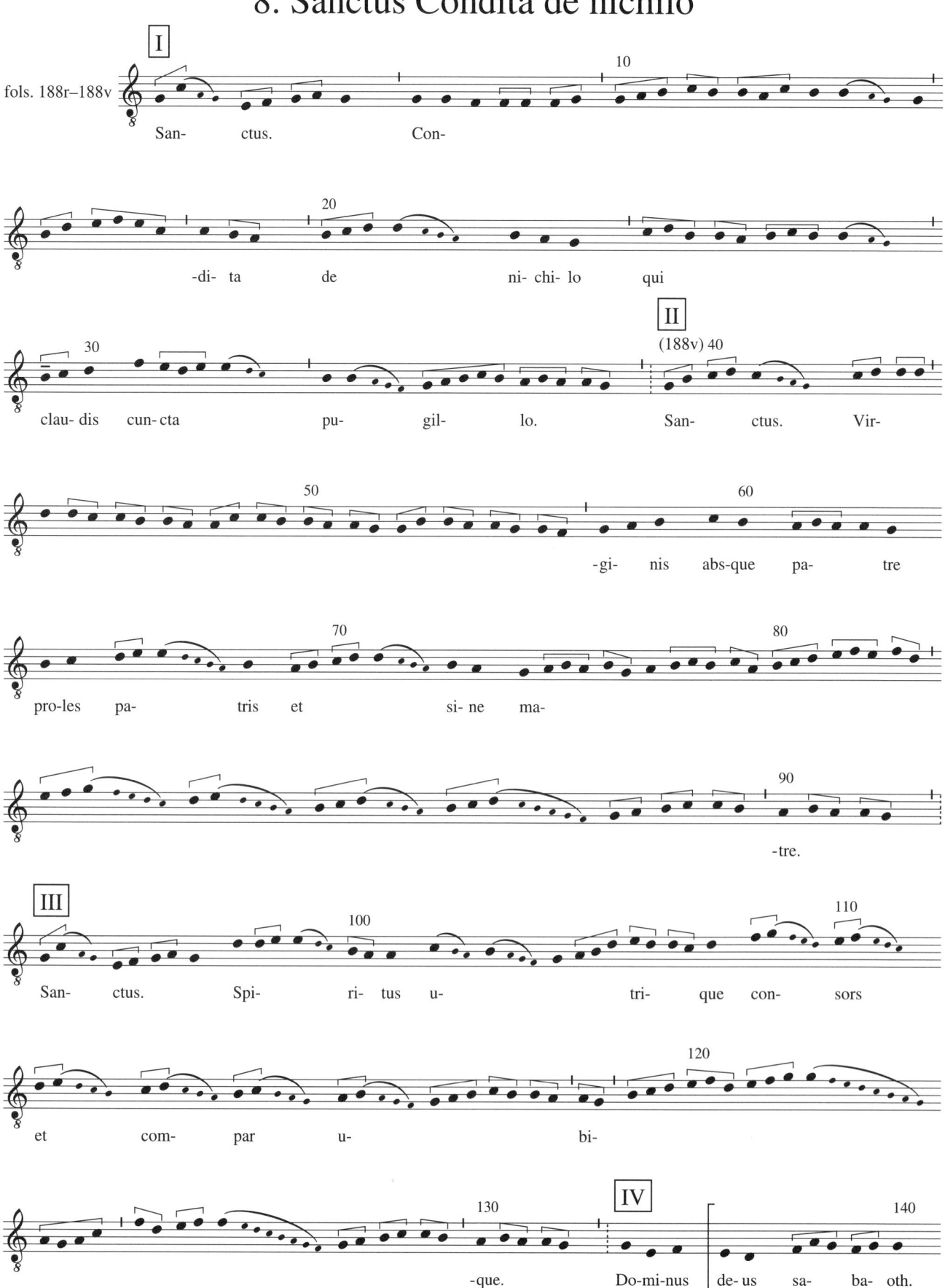

fols. 188r–188v

Sanctus. Condita de nichilo qui claudis cuncta pugillo. Sanctus. Virginis absque patre proles patris et sine matre. Sanctus. Spiritus utrique consors et compar ubique. Dominus deus sabaoth.

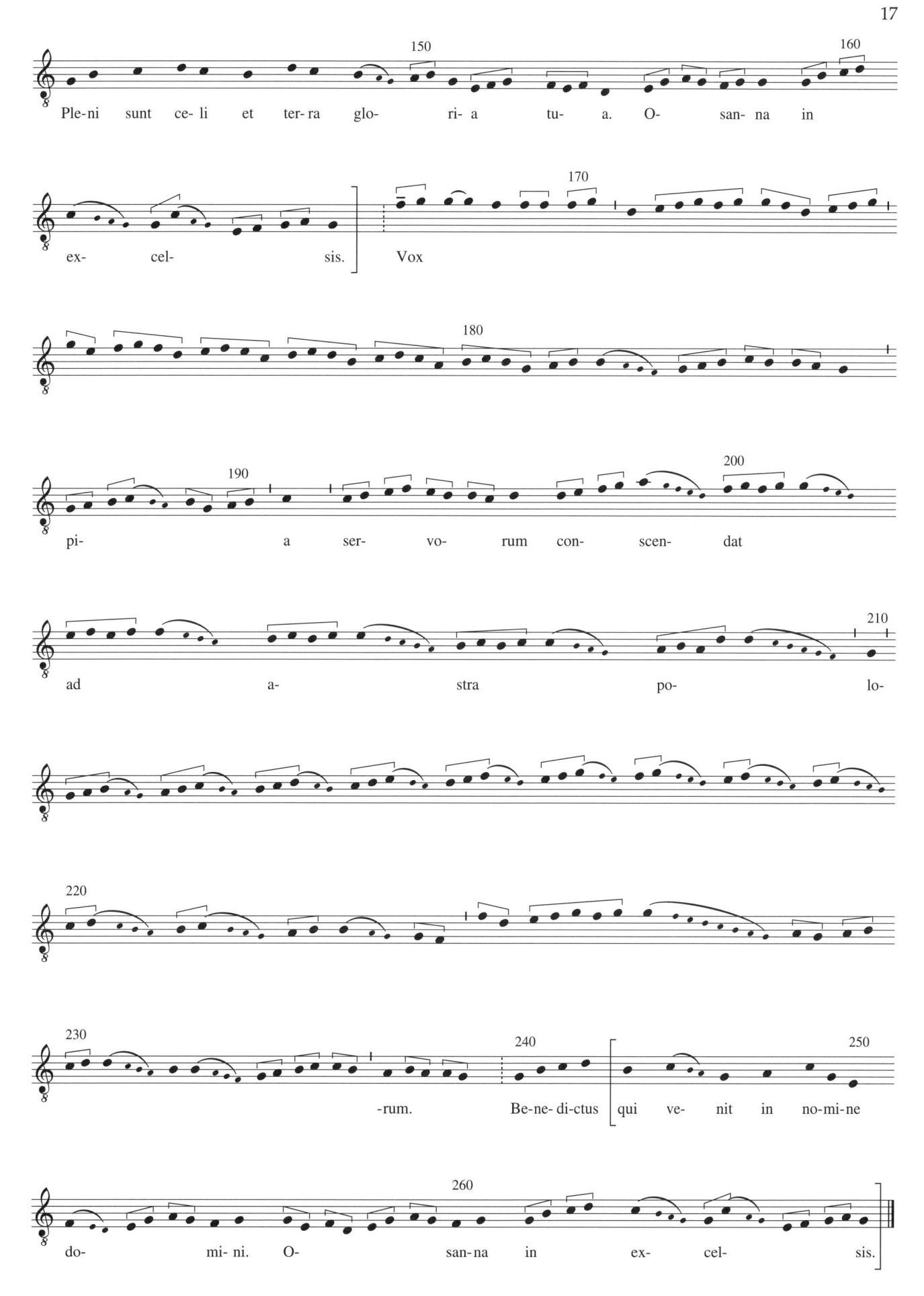

Ple-ni sunt ce- li et ter- ra glo- ri- a tu- a. O- san- na in ex- cel- sis. Vox pi- a ser- vo- rum con- scen- dat ad a- stra po- lo- -rum. Be-ne- di-ctus qui ve- nit in no-mi-ne do- mi- ni. O- san- na in ex- cel- sis.

9. Sanctus Sanctus ab eterno

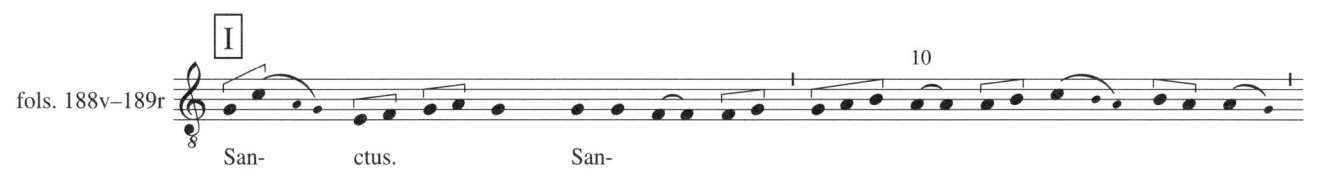

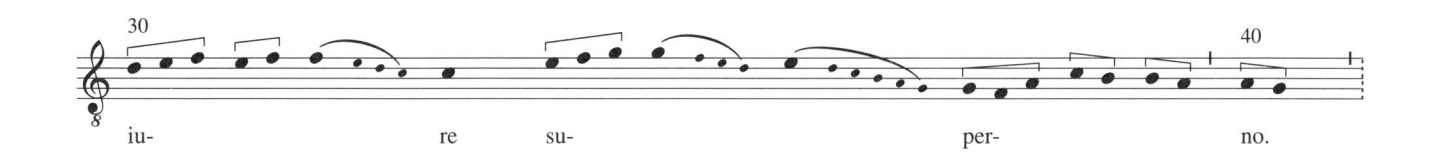

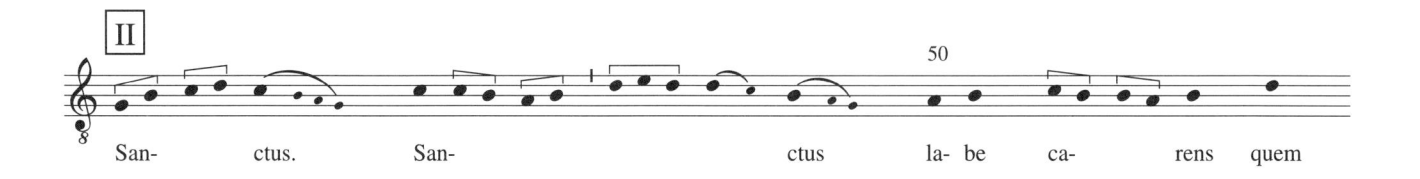

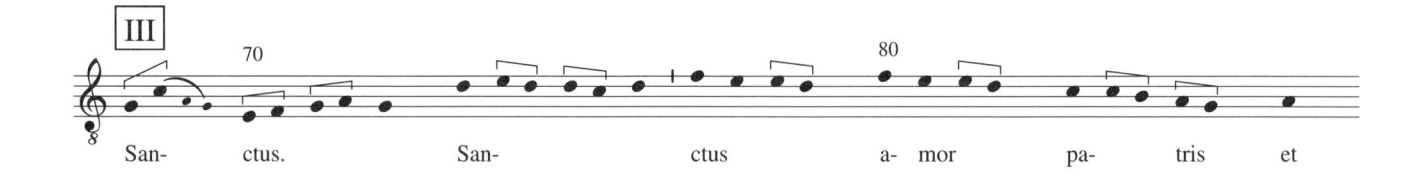

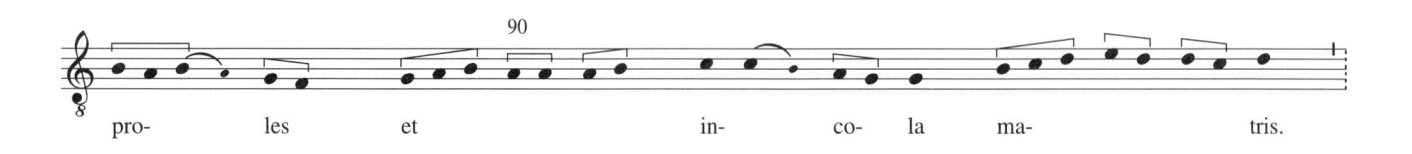

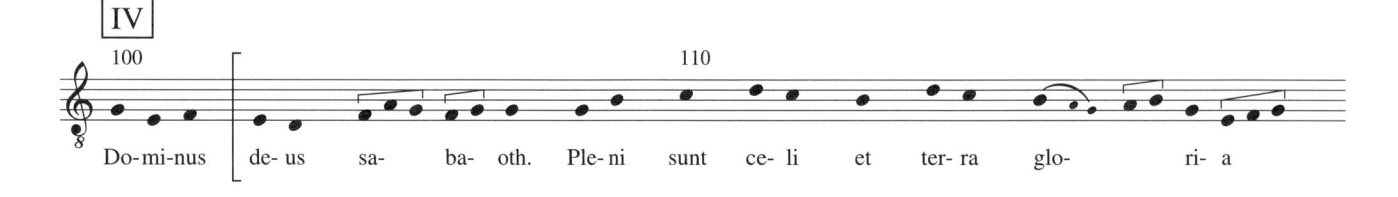

fols. 188v–189r

Sanctus. Sanctus ab eterno rex regum iure superno.

Sanctus. Sanctus labe carens quem parit alma parens.

Sanctus. Sanctus amor patris et proles et incola matris.

Dominus deus sabaoth. Pleni sunt celi et terra gloria

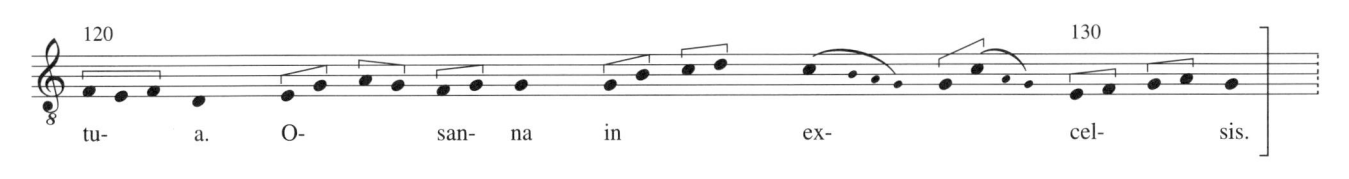

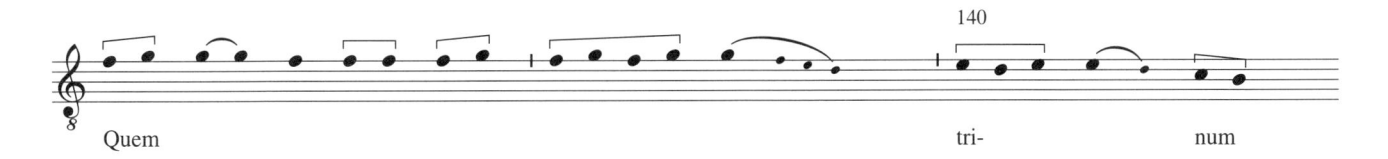

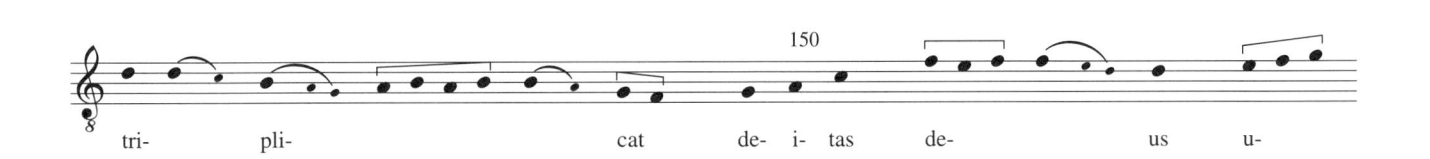

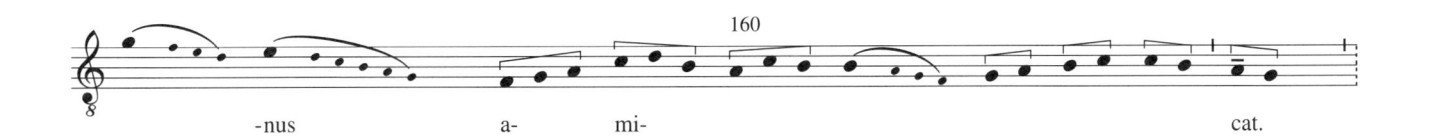

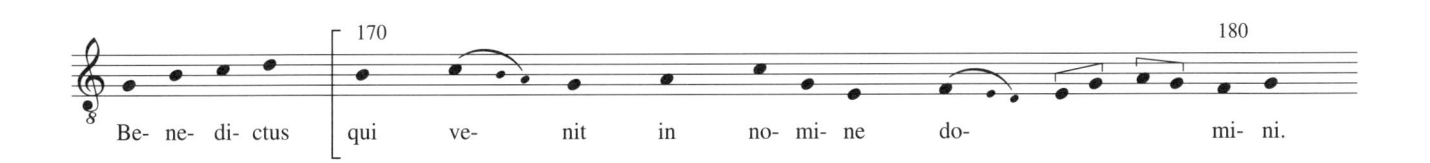

tu- a. O- san- na in ex- cel- sis.

Quem tri- num

tri- pli- cat de- i- tas de- us u-

-nus a- mi- cat.

Be- ne- di- ctus qui ve- nit in no- mi- ne do- mi- ni.

O- san- na in ex- cel- sis.

Agnus Tropes
10. Agnus Archetipi mundi

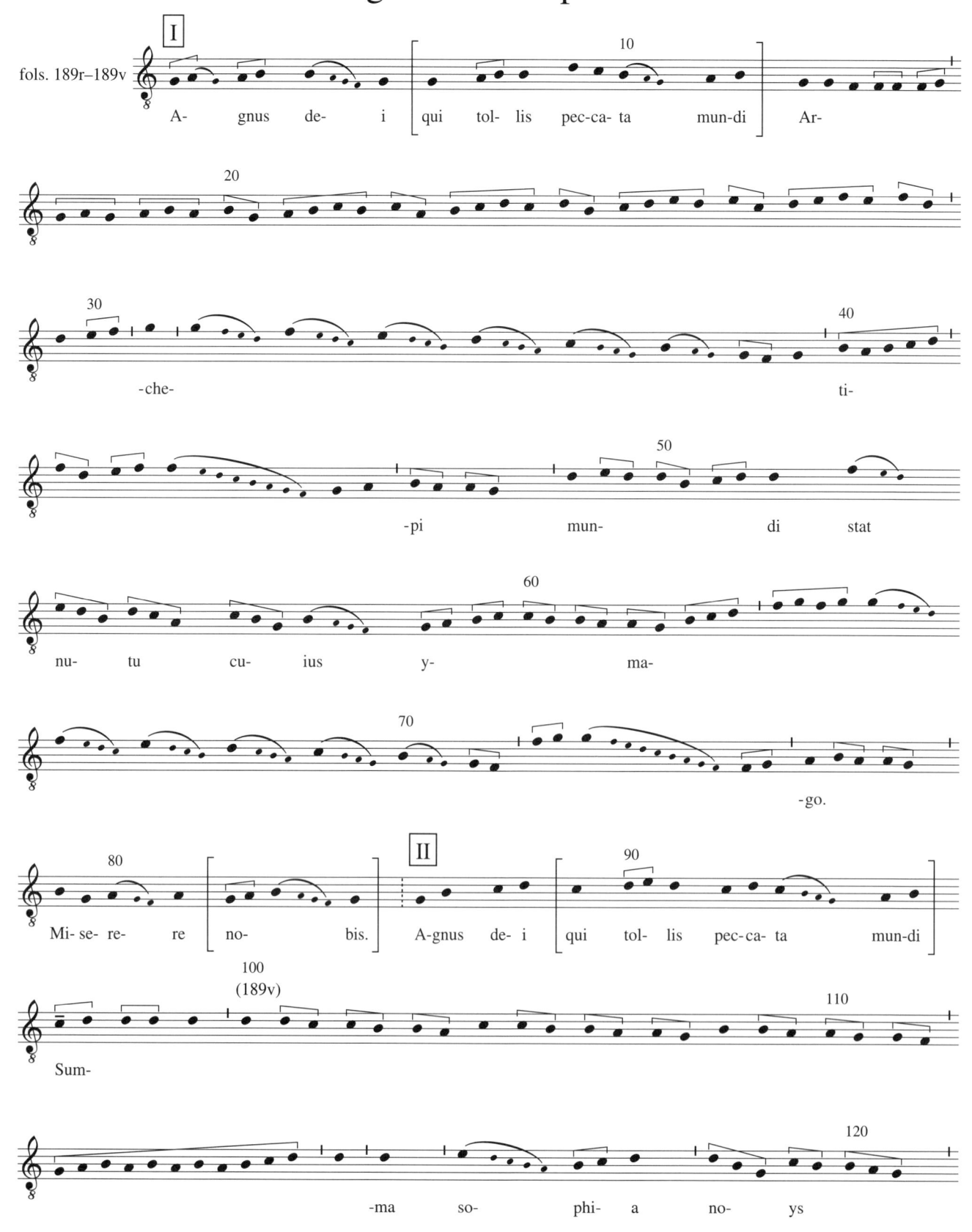

fols. 189r–189v

A- gnus de- i qui tol- lis pec-ca- ta mun-di Ar- -che- ti- -pi mun- di stat nu- tu cu- ius y- ma- -go. Mi- se- re- re no- bis. A-gnus de- i qui tol- lis pec-ca- ta mun-di Sum- -ma so- phi- a no- ys

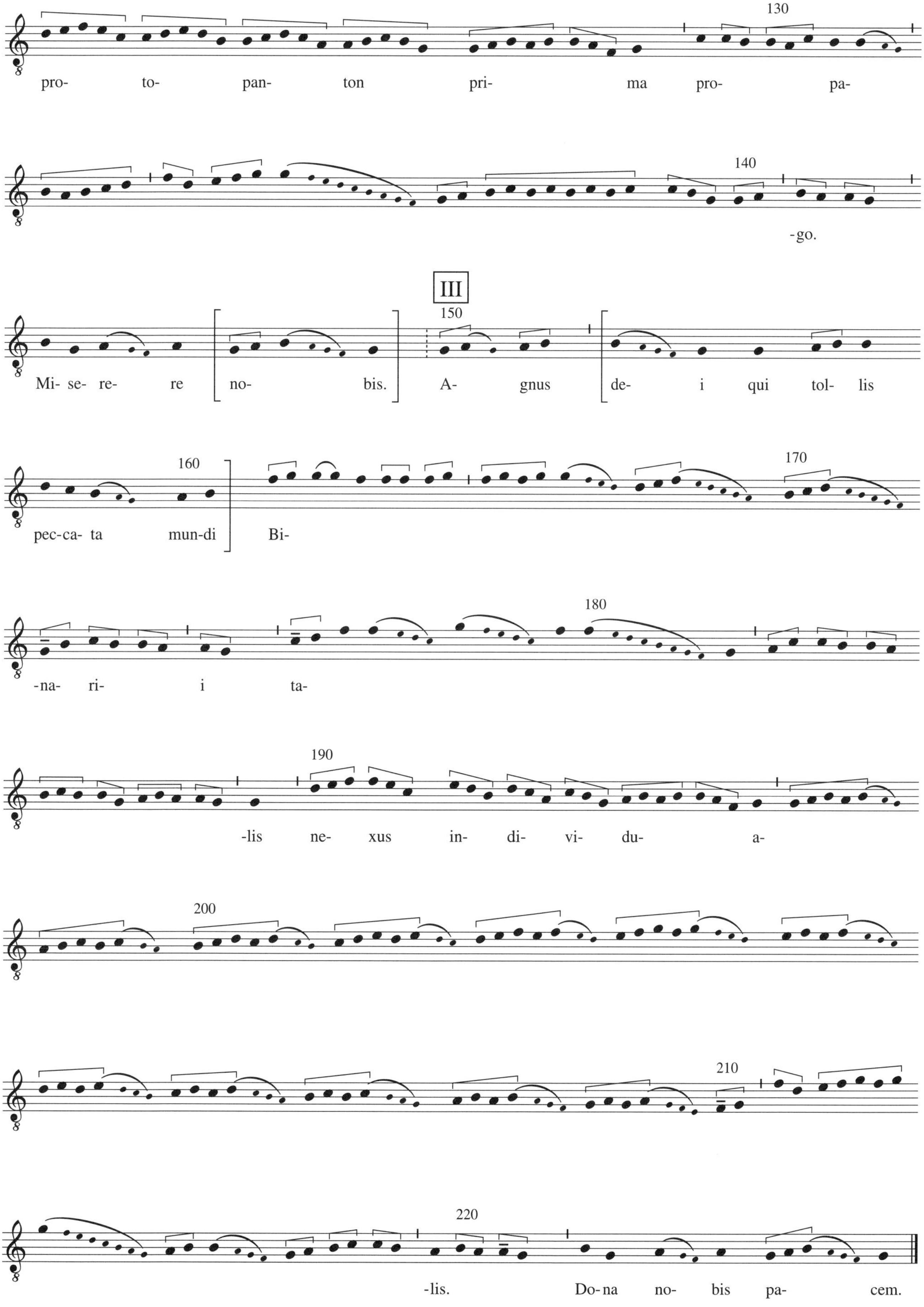
pro- to- pan- ton pri- ma pro- pa-
-go.
III
Mi- se- re- re no- bis. A- gnus de- i qui tol- lis
pec-ca- ta mun-di Bi-
-na- ri- i ta-
-lis ne- xus in- di- vi- du- a-
-lis. Do-na no- bis pa- cem.

11. Agnus Pectoris alta

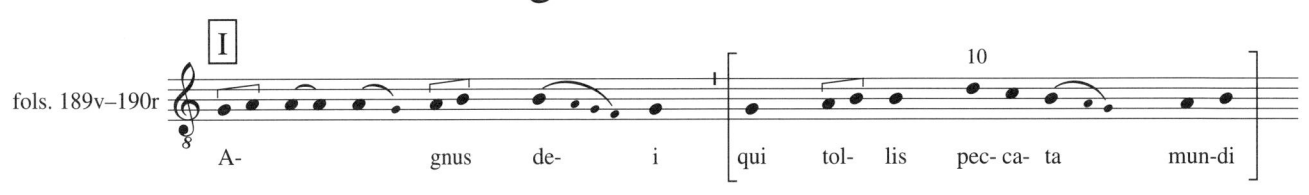

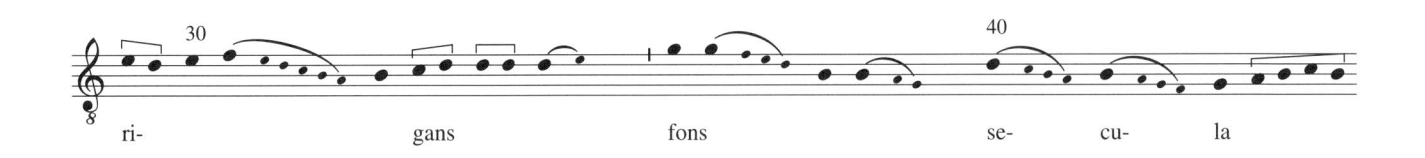

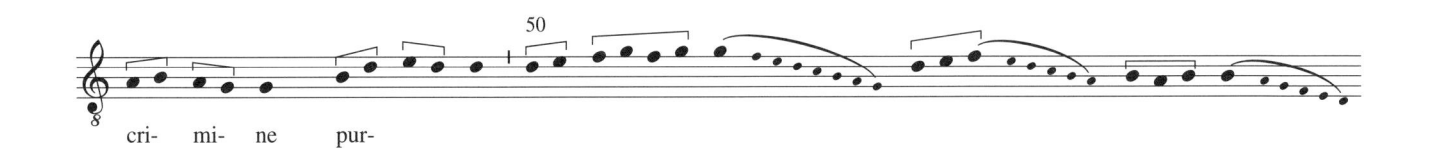

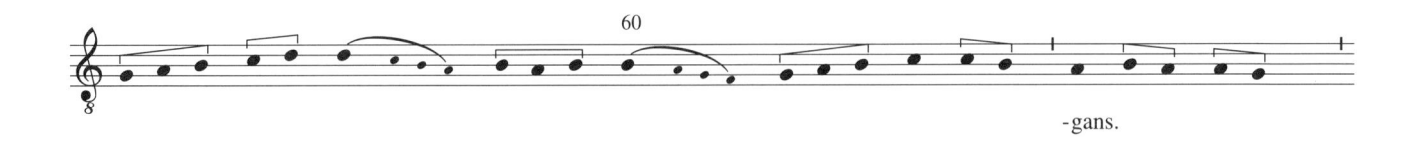

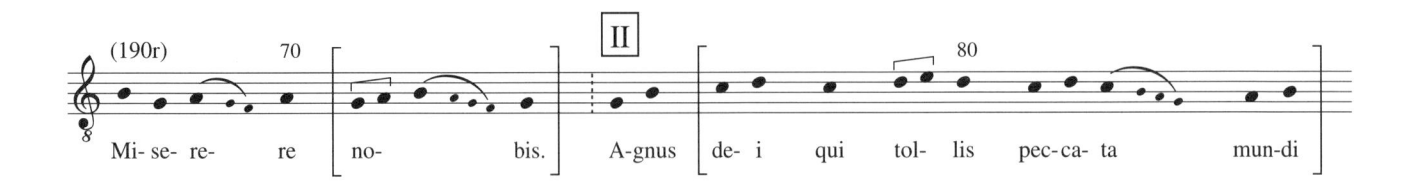

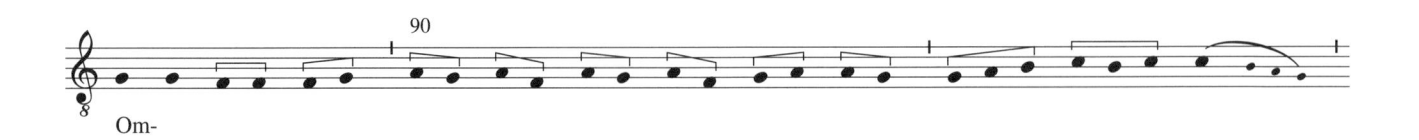

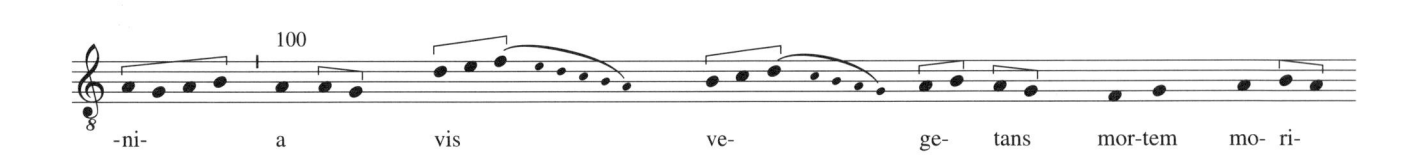

fols. 189v–190r

A- gnus de- i qui tol- lis pec-ca- ta mun-di

Pe- cto- ris al- ta

ri- gans fons se- cu- la

cri- mi- ne pur-

-gans.

(190r) Mi- se- re- re no- bis. A-gnus de- i qui tol- lis pec-ca- ta mun-di

Om-

-ni- a vis ve- ge- tans mor-tem mo- ri-

110 120
-en- do re-

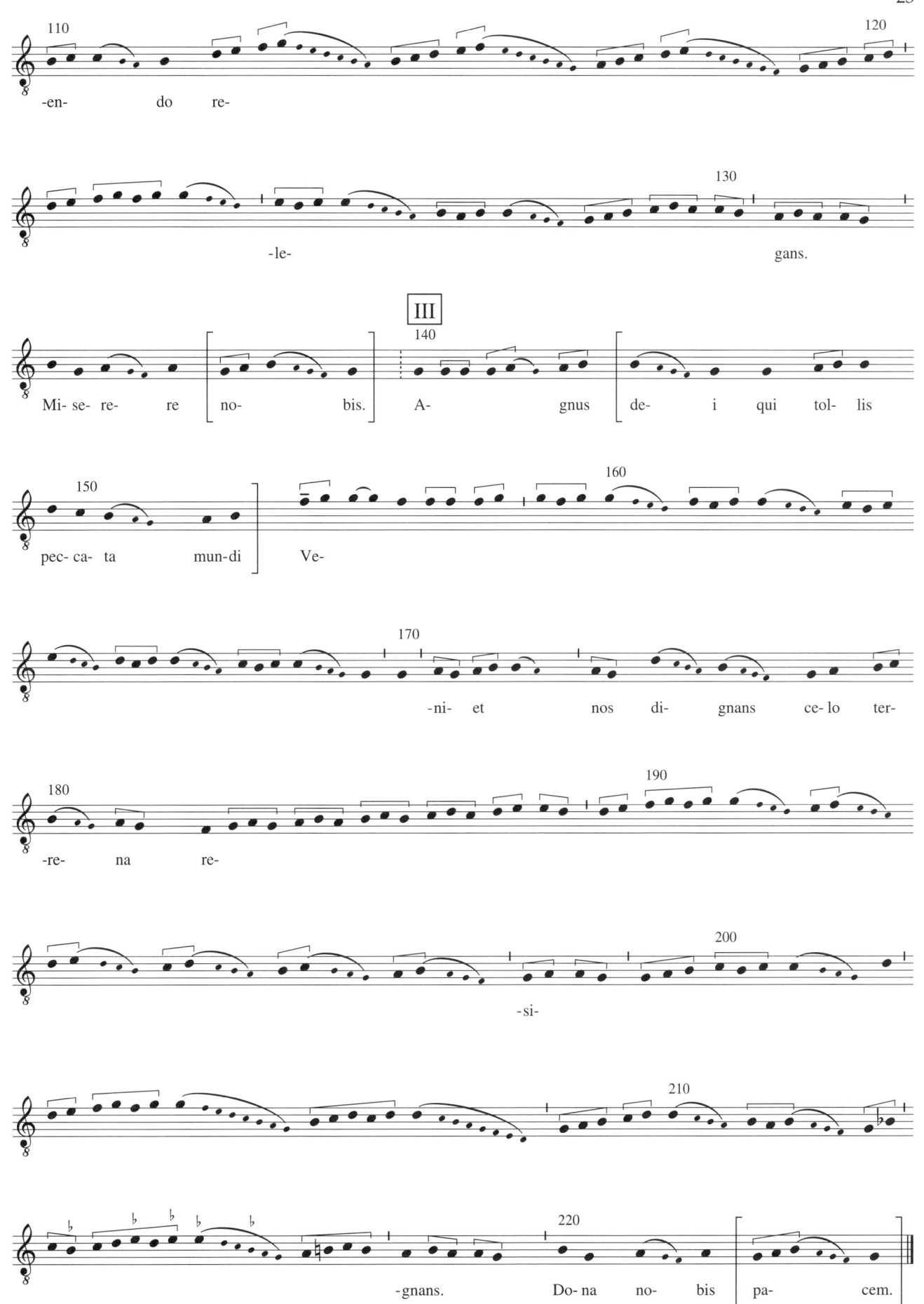

130
-le- gans.

III
140
Mi- se- re- re no- bis. A- gnus de- i qui tol- lis

150 160
pec- ca- ta mun-di Ve-

170
-ni- et nos di- gnans ce- lo ter-

180 190
-re- na re-

200
-si-

210

220
-gnans. Do- na no- bis pa- cem.

12. Agnus Qui de virgineo

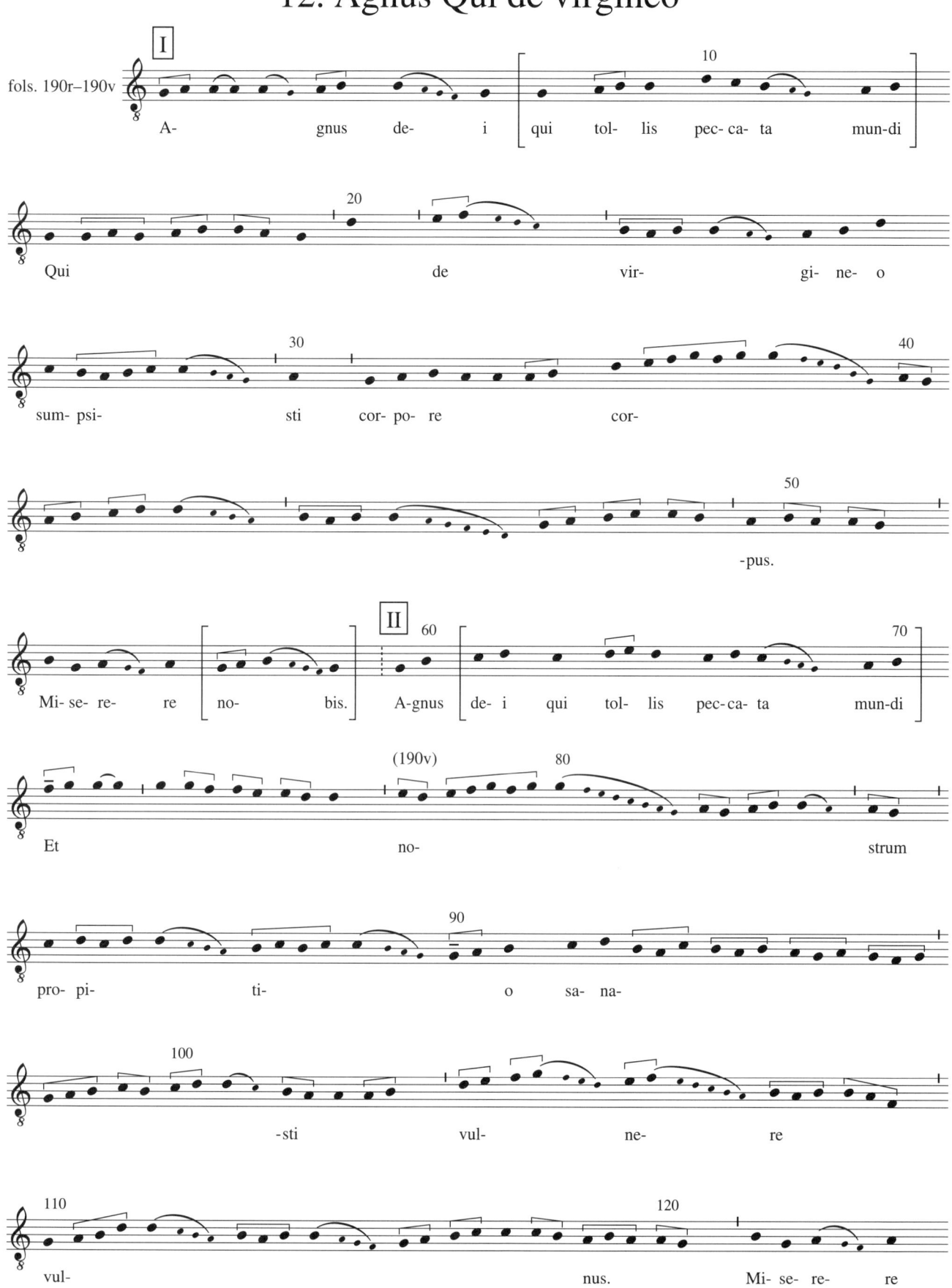

no- bis. A- gnus de- i qui tol- lis pec-ca- ta mun-di

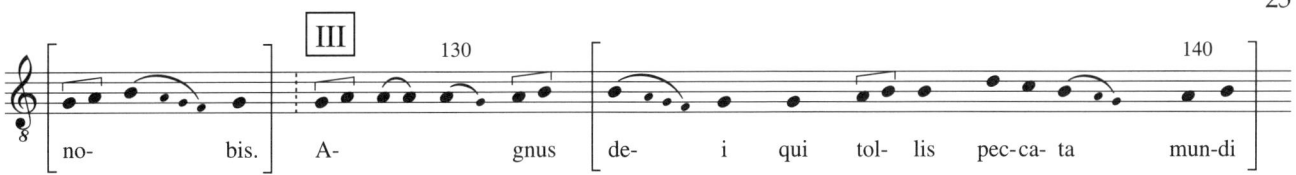

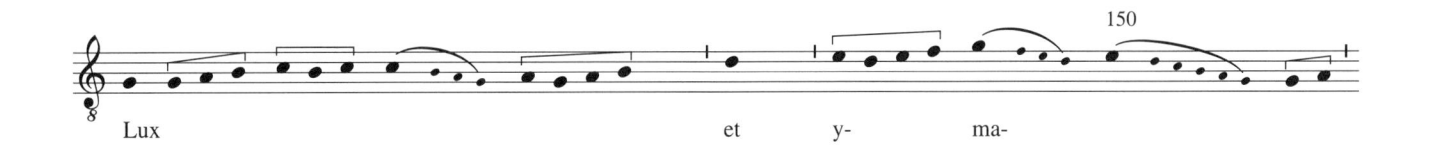

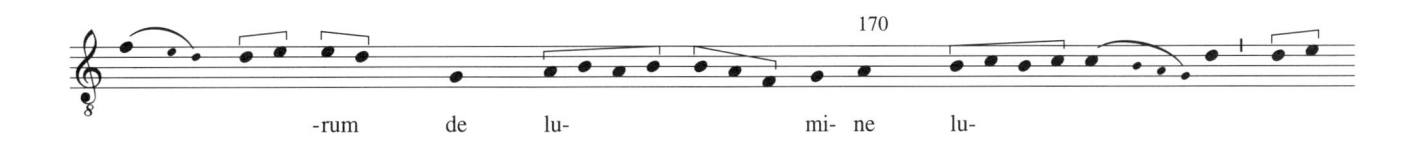

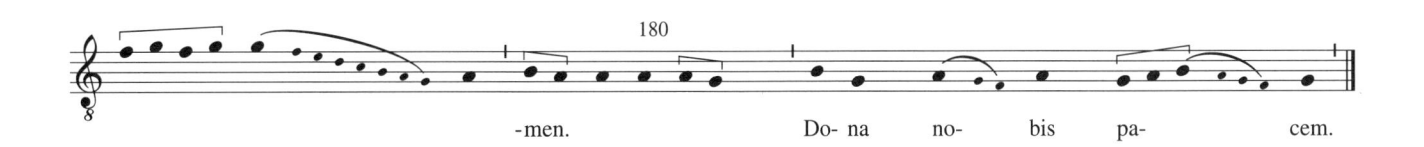

Lux et y- ma-

-go pa- tris ve-

-rum de lu- mi- ne lu-

-men. Do- na no- bis pa- cem.

13. Agnus Lux lucis

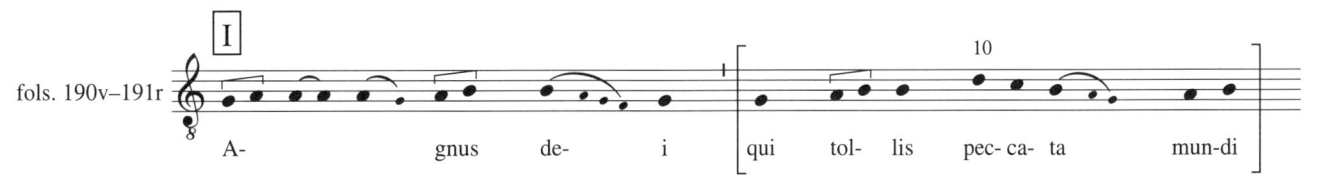

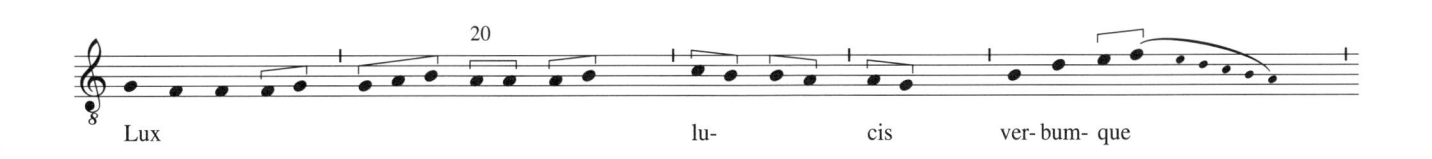

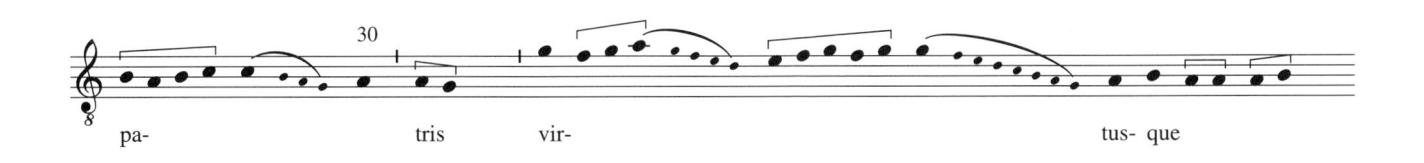

fols. 190v–191r

A- gnus de- i qui tol- lis pec-ca- ta mun-di

Lux lu- cis ver-bum- que

pa- tris vir- tus- que

per- hen- nis. Mi- se- re- re no- bis.

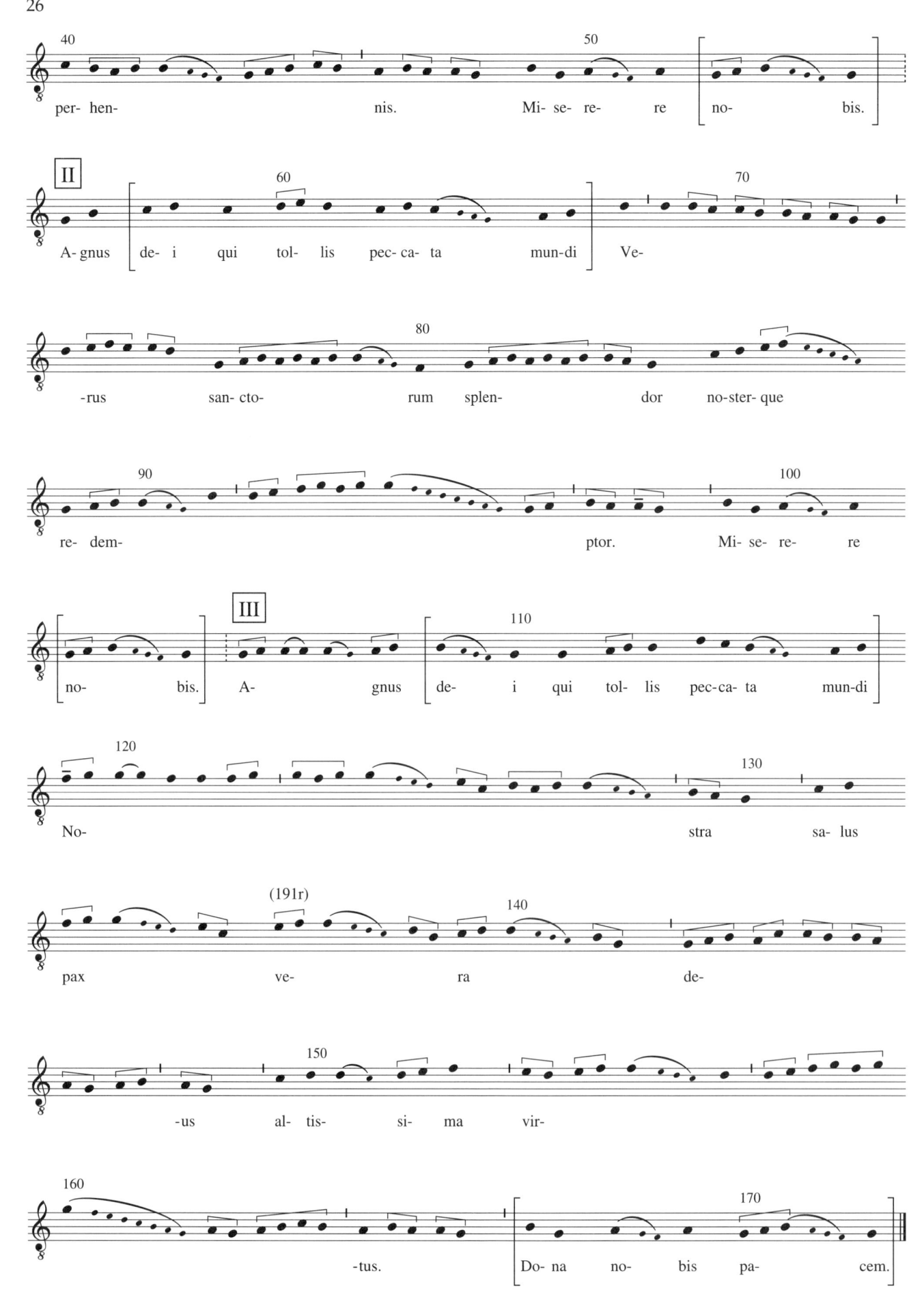

II A- gnus de- i qui tol- lis pec-ca- ta mun-di Ve-

-rus san- cto- rum splen- dor no-ster- que

re- dem- ptor. Mi- se- re- re

III no- bis. A- gnus de- i qui tol- lis pec-ca- ta mun-di

No- stra sa- lus

pax ve- ra de-

-us al- tis- si- ma vir-

-tus. Do- na no- bis pa- cem.

14. Agnus Humano generi

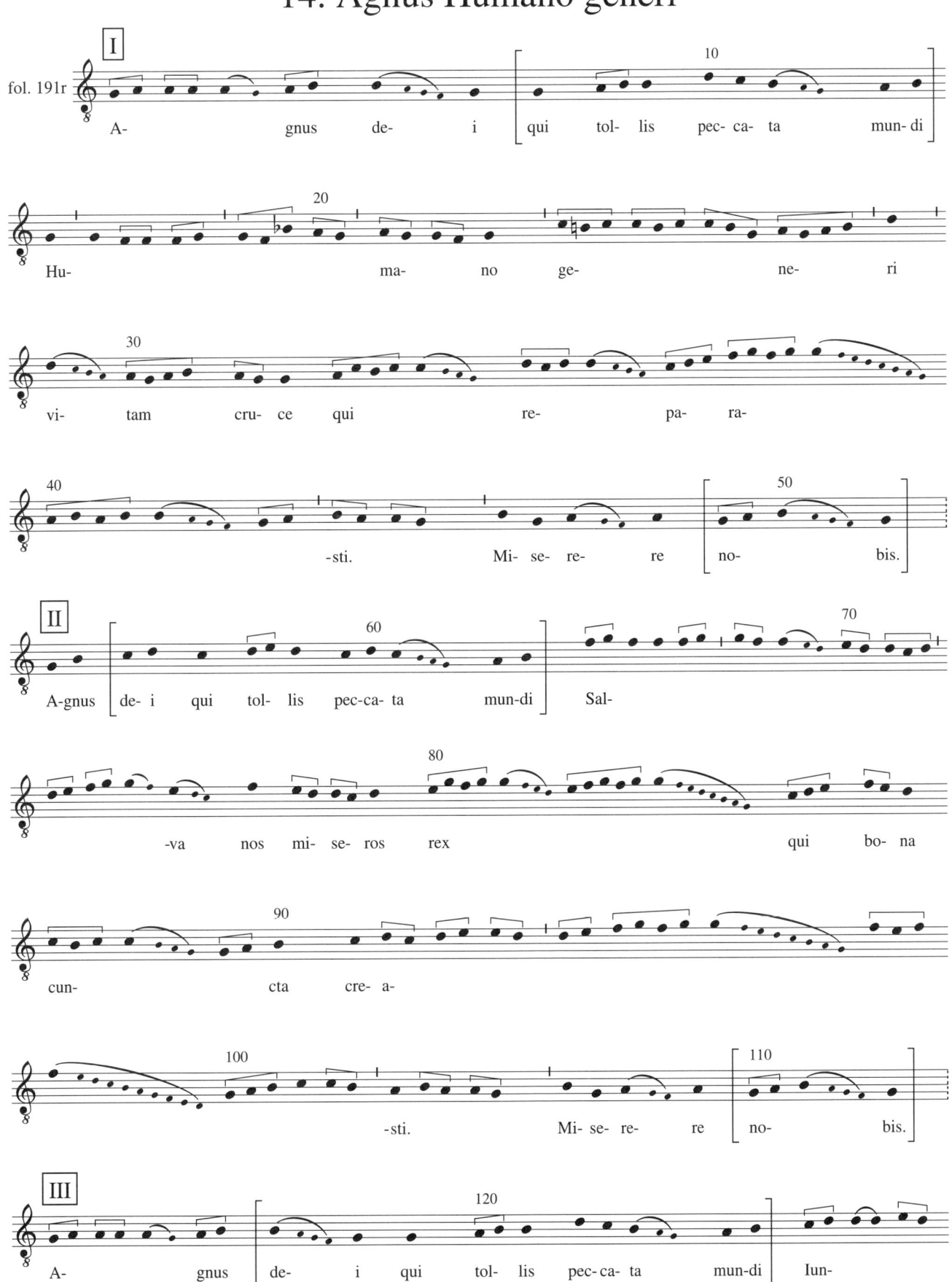

28

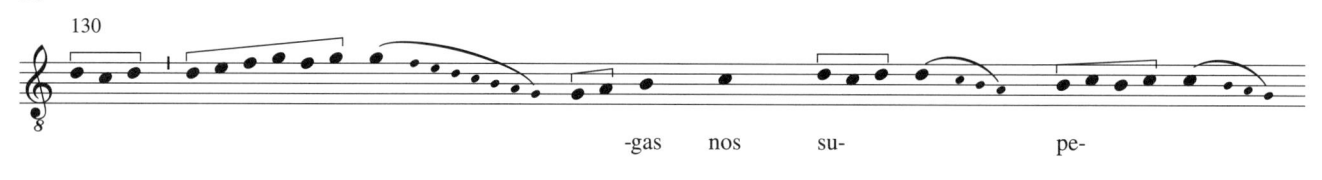

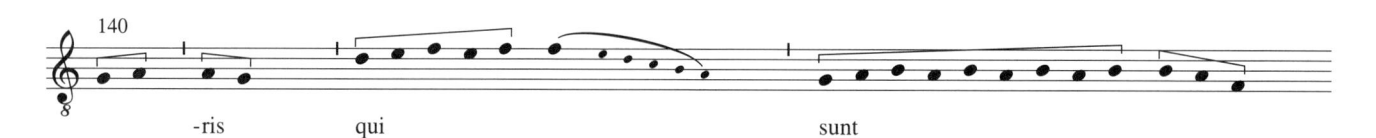

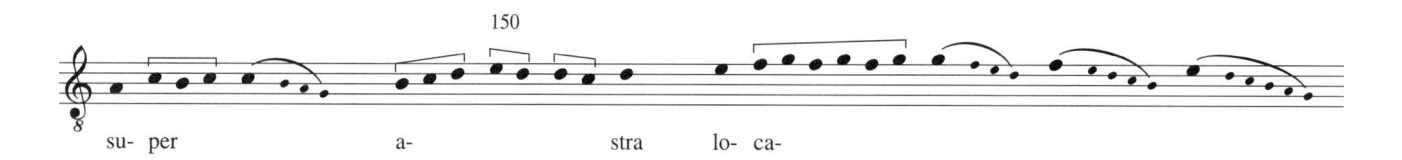

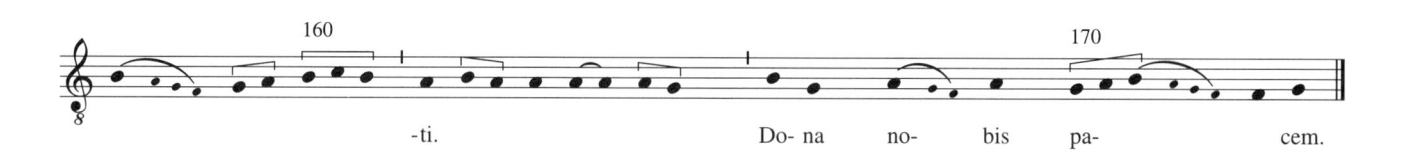

15. Agnus Vulnere quorum

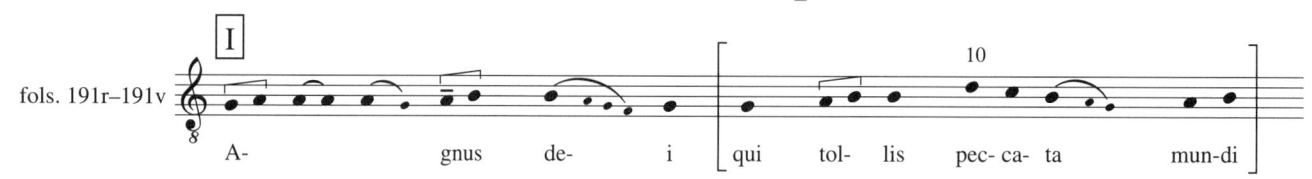

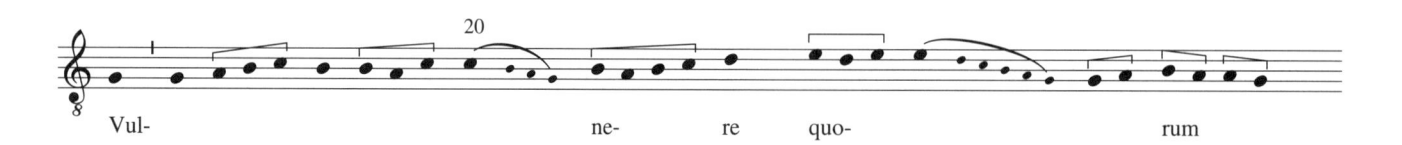

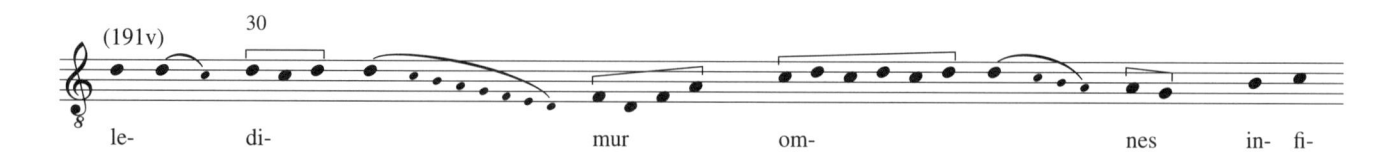

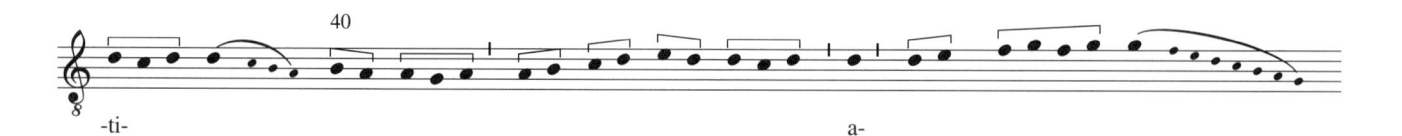

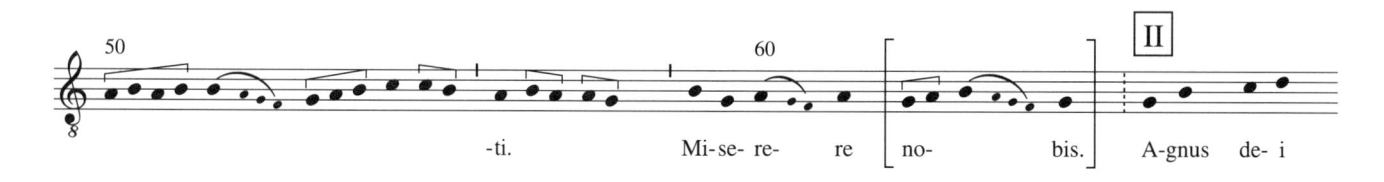

29

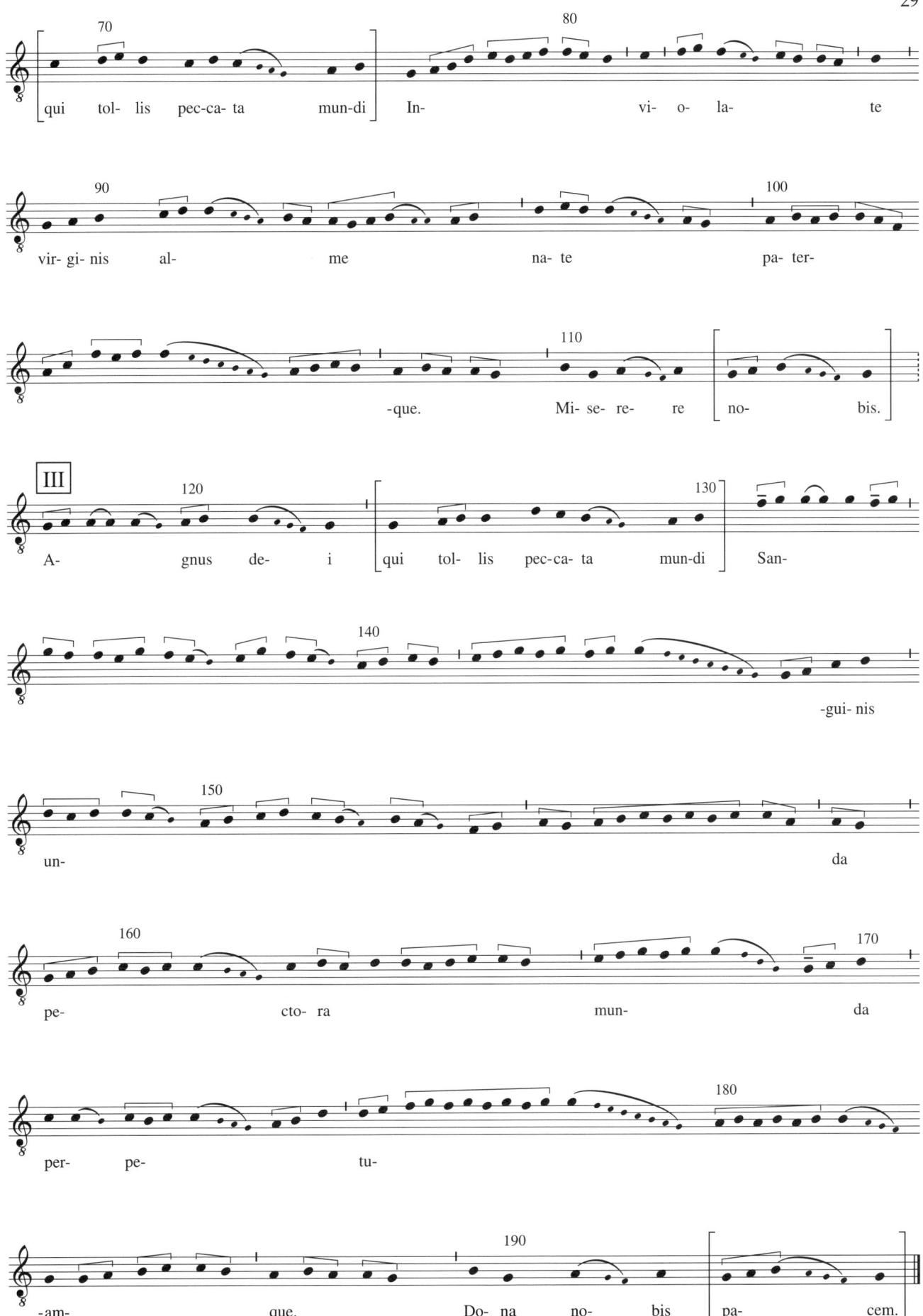

[qui tol-lis pec-ca-ta mun-di] In- vi- o- la- te vir-gi-nis al- me na- te pa-ter- -que. Mi-se-re- re [no- bis.]

III A-gnus de- i [qui tol-lis pec-ca-ta mun-di] San- -gui-nis un- da pe- cto- ra mun- da per- pe- tu- -am- que. Do- na no- bis [pa- cem.]

Critical Report

Editorial Methods

This edition aims to represent the manuscript as faithfully as possible while making the music accessible to the modern reader. All significant editorial alterations or additions are bracketed or have been documented in the critical notes. Each composition is newly numbered to reflect its appearance in the fascicle. Folio numbers are given at the opening of each piece and at internal page turns. According to modern scholarly custom, the music is notated in stemless black noteheads set in transposing treble clef. It should be noted that the pitches indicated by the medieval C clefs are only relative, so performers may treat the register with some flexibility. Internal clef changes from third-, fourth-, or second-line C clefs in the manuscript are incorporated into the transcription without comment. In the tropes, roman numerals above the staff show the beginnings of sections (see table 2). Throughout the edition, editorial dashed barlines mark the ends of sections, subsections, and poetic lines. The end of each piece is marked by an editorial final barline.

Repeated single pitches are often written in a combination of note shapes: virga, square puncta, or rhomboid notes. In the edition, virgas are always transcribed as isolated notes, while other repeated notes are grouped together in some way. Series of repeated pitches most often feature rhomboidal shapes, but they also occur in various gradations of more square forms, especially at phrase beginnings. Shapes that are clearly rhomboidal are grouped under a slur, while the quadratic forms are marked with a bracket. Given that the difference between the two forms is sometimes subtle, readers should consult the facsimile to see the actual note shapes.

In addition to single noteheads, W1 scribes indicate a variety of note groupings and melodic figures. Quadratic-shaped ligature groups are transcribed with brackets, while rhomboidal currentes are indicated with slurs. A descending run of currentes is represented as a main note followed by smaller notes, all under a slur. Many times currentes elide with a ligature; this is shown by slurring the last note in a bracketed group to the following currentes. A note or ligature drawn with an elongated stroke in the manuscript is indicated by a tenuto line over the note in the edition. A plica is represented by a small slur touching both the antecedent and the plicated note, which is given in miniature. Although some of the ligature groupings suggest viable rhythmic interpretation in modal rhythm, the preceding discussion shows that these possibilities must be regarded as tentative (see "Notes on Performance" in the introduction). Thus, the material is left unmeasured so that performers can make their own decisions.

In the original, the tracti are placed in the staff, drawn through approximately one space and part of the adjacent lines, in the location where the musical phrase has just been completed. In the edition they are always drawn at the top of the staff. Accidentals printed on the staff without brackets are those appearing in the original manuscript. One accidental is placed in brackets in *Sanctus Rex qui cuncta regis* (no. 5); it is taken from similar passages in other tropes (see the critical notes for details). All inflections precede the beginning of a ligature group in the source. In the edition, they are placed immediately preceding the altered note, according to modern convention, and are valid only for one note or ligature group. Musica ficta above the staff are editorial suggestions and are valid only for the note above which they appear. Passages in large brackets are those portions of the parent chants that have been supplied by the editor. (See "Tropes: Parent Chants" in the introduction for a detailed discussion, and complete transcriptions in the appendix.)

Text underlay is set according to the syllable placement in the manuscript, where cues of tractus and ligature help place text in a relatively clear manner. Any underlay that is questionable is noted in the critical notes. Syllables are divided according to the modern standard hyphenation scheme of the *Liber Usualis* and other sources for singing in Latin, which differ at times from the syllable divisions indicated by the W1 scribe. Readers may wish to note these differences, recorded in the critical notes, as they may indicate nuances of dialect or region. Initial letters are sometimes missing in the source and are added tacitly in the underlaid text. For information about orthography and adjustments in spelling, including missing initial letters, see the notes in the "Texts and Translations."

Critical Notes

Critical notes include three categories: (1) "Catalog references" cite the location of the piece in modern reference catalogs by volume (when applicable) and identification number; (2) "Concordances" list concordant manuscript sources (sigla are given in full citations at the beginning of this volume); (3) "Notes" record significant corrections or alterations made to the original. Notes are cued to reference numbers added to the music, counting each notational element (virga, punctum, currentes group, ligature) as a single item. Pitches are identified with capital letters without reference to a particular octave.

In addition to manuscript sigla listed at the front of the volume, the following abbreviations appear in the critical notes:

AH	Guido Maria Dreves, Clemens Blume, and Henry Marriott Bannister, eds., *Analecta hymnica medii aevi*, 55 vols. (Leipzig: Reisland, 1886–1922).
Falck	Robert Falck, *The Notre Dame Conductus: A Study of the Repertory* (Ottowa: Institute of Medieval Music, 1981).
Thannabaur	Peter Josef Thannabaur, *Das einstimmige Sanctus der römischen Messe in der handschriftlichen Überlieferung des 11. bis 16. Jahrhunderts*, Erlanger Arbeiten zur Musikwissenschaft, no. 1 (München: Walter Ricke, 1962).
Schildbach	Martin Schildbach, "Das einstimmige Agnus Dei und seine handschriftliche Überlieferung vom 10. bis zum 16. Jahrhundert" (Ph.D. diss., Friedrich-Alexander-Universität, 1967).
CT IV	Gunilla Iversen, *Corpus Troporum IV: Tropes de l'Agnus Dei*, Studia Latina Stockholmiensia, vol. 26 (Stockholm: Almqvist & Wiksell International, 1980).
CT VII	Gunilla Iversen, *Corpus Troporum VII: Tropes du Sanctus; Tropes de l'ordinaire de la messe*, Studia Latina Stockholmiensia, vol. 34 (Stockholm: Almqvist & Wiksell International, 1990).

1. *Quomodo cantabimus*

Catalog references.   AH 21:165, Falck 296.

Concordances.   F (425v–426r), Da (21r), Fauv (32r).

Notes.   **1–37:** Lacuna in W1; music and text are from F, fol. 425v.   **5:** B♭ is notated at beginning of only the opening line along with the clef in F.

2. *Ve mundo a scandalis*

Catalog references.   AH 21:148, Falck 356.

Concordances.   F (426r–426v), Da (6r), Hu (157v–158r), Sab (142r), Tours (14r).

Notes.   B♭ key signature on every line.   **138:** An additional tractus before this note in F makes it clear that "quo" starts on element 138.

3. *In Rama sonat gemitus*

Catalog reference.   Falck 181.

Notes.   **31:** Lower case *i* is dotted with a long slash mark, which lies on the staff and could be confused for a plica or a note.   **58:** Only example of F clef in Fascicle X.

4. *Sanctus Christe yerarchia*

Notes.   **27–29:** The scribe continues the musical phrase into the margin; the last three elements are off the staff.   **154:** Text divided "cu-i," with the second part of the dipthong set under 175.   **183–84:** Music written off the staff in the margin.   **240–42:** The notes written for "sabaoth" are a variant of the melody given in PBN 1112. This is the only trope in Fascicle X that has notes for "sabaoth" written out; therefore, these notes serve as a template for the missing chant in the following tropes.   **297–98:** Music written off the staff in the margin.   **305:** Second note could be E or F; E is most likely, as the scribe tends to sit notes on the line.   **317–21:** Plicas here could be interpreted stepwise or down a third from the main note.   **343:** Third note reaches below the staff at an indeterminate interval; D fits best with the mode.

5. *Sanctus Rex qui cuncta regis*

Catalog references.   AH 47:262, Thannabaur 185, CT VII 133.

Concordances.   SG 378 (p. 380), SG 383 (p. 246), SG 546 (80v).

Notes.   **53:** Second note unclear; A fits best with the melody and mode.   **119:** Second note reaches below the staff at an indeterminate interval; D fits best with the mode. **222:** First note is on the B line but written very high; it seems C is intended. **229:** The editorial ♮ is taken from similar cadences in *Sanctus Omnia qui libras* (no. 6), on the word "telum," and *Agnus Pecoris alta* (no. 11), on the word "resignans."

6. *Sanctus Omnia qui libras*

Catalog references. AH 47:261, Thannabaur 123, *CT* VII 81.

Concordances. Bar 1408/9 (2r), PBN 2298 (39r), SG 383 (pp. 246–47), SG 546 (80v), St-M C (31v–32v).

Notes. **64:** No clef at the beginning of this line; surrounding clefs and melodic formulae indicate that it should be C3. **112:** The ♮ sign appears to have been misplaced; it is placed at the end of the phrase, after 115, but there are no notes B following the sign. A similar cadential formula is found in *Agnus Pectoris alta* (no. 11) on the word "resignans." There the natural is placed before the ligature A–B–C–B. This placement is used in the present passage. **116–20:** The notes written for "Sanctus" are partially worn away. It appears as if the music scribe wrote the melody for the second "Sanctus," then realized his mistake and scraped off the notes. The correct melody for the third "Sanctus" iteration can be surmised from the other tropes. **167:** Note is F, but it is written very low on the staff. The scribe was probably avoiding a collision with the text; E agrees with the other tropes.

7. *Sanctus Cunctorum dominans*

Catalog reference. Thannabaur 47.

Note. **150 and 193:** Ink blots at the end of the staff seem to be from the facing folio (187v).

8. *Sanctus Condita de nichilo*

Catalog reference. Thannabaur 34.

Notes. **36:** Ligature crowded before a hole in the manuscript leaf. (The hole was there before the scribes used the leaf.) **56:** Text syllable "-gi-" is set below the following note.

9. *Sanctus Sanctus ab eterno*

Catalog reference. Thannabaur 2.

10. *Agnus Archetipi mundi*

Catalog references. AH 47:398, Schildbach 9.

Concordances. This text does not appear elsewhere as an Agnus trope; *AH* 47:398 gives SG 383 as a concordance for *Agnus Archetipi mundi* without explanation, perhaps because it shares its text with *Sanctus Archetipi mundi*. This related Sanctus survives in the following manuscripts: PBN 3126 (9r), SG 383 (pp. 255–56), and SG 546 (81v).

Note. **118–19:** Text correction of "noys" (for "nobis") underlaid as two syllables following scribe's underlay of "nobis."

11. *Agnus Pectoris alta*

Catalog reference. Schildbach 83.

Notes. **15–24:** Text division is "Pec-to-." **214–15:** E♭ ficta follows similar cadential formula in *Sanctus Omnia qui libras* (no. 6) and *Sanctus Rex qui cuncta regis* (no. 5).

12. *Agnus Qui de virgineo*

Catalog reference. Schildbach 94.

Notes. **1–4:** Text division is "Ag-nus." This division is also written for the initial "Agnus" in all subsequent tropes in Fascicle X. **27–28:** Text division is "sump-si-." **39:** It is unusual to see currentes that do not descend stepwise; this only occurs once more in Fascicle X (*Agnus Vulnere quorum* [no. 15]). **94:** Unclear spacing of second note in oblique ligature; following sequence suggests A.

13. *Agnus Lux lucis*

Catalog references. AH 47:387, Schildbach 55, *CT* IV 34.

Concordances. Assisi 695 (51r), DeZayas (3r), Du 6 (*CT* IV), Iv 60 (101r), Lo 13 (*AH*, *CT* IV), Lo 2B.IV (*AH*), Ma 288 (158r), Ma 289 (98r–98v), Ma 19421 (96v), OxB 775 (*AH*, *CT* IV), OxB b5 (89v), PBA 135 (287r), PBN 1235 (201r–201v, 218v, 226r [incomplete]), PBN 3126 (78r), PBN 7185 (*CT* IV), PBN 9449 (20r–20v, 48v, 56v), PBN 10508 (127v), PBN 10511 (323r), Wor 160 (*AH*), W1 (93v).

Note. **166–67:** The word "Dona" is written in the margin, but there is no music for this cue.

14. *Agnus Humano generi*

Catalog reference. Schildbach 47.

Note. **171:** The repetition of the note F is not found in the other tropes; although it seems to be placed intentionally.

15. *Agnus Vulnere quorum*

Catalog references. AH 47:440, Schildbach 138.

Concordances. Assisi 695 (50r), La 263 (84r), Li 2(17) (254r–254v), PBN 3126 (77v), SL HB I.95 (43r). Another trope, *Agnus Vulnere mortis*, contains virtually the same text and is found in the following manuscripts: Berlin 40171 (Schildbach), SG 382 (later addition).

Notes. **159–62:** Text division is "pec-to-." **168:** It is unusual to see currentes that do not descend stepwise. **177:** Text underlay moved from 176 because of tractus and similar text underlay patterns elsewhere.

Appendix

Sanctus
PBN 1112

San- ctus. San- ctus. San- ctus. Do- mi- nus de- us sa- ba- oth. Ple- ni sunt ce- li et ter- ra glo- -ri- a tu- a. O- san- na in ex- cel- sis. Be- ne- di- ctus qui ve- nit in no- mi- ne do- mi- ni. O- san- na in ex- cel- sis.

Sanctus
Reconstructed from W1

San- ctus. San- ctus. San- ctus. Do- mi- nus de- us sa- ba- oth. Ple- ni sunt ce- li et ter- ra glo- -ri- a tu- a. O- san- na in ex- cel- -sis. Be- ne- di- ctus qui ve- nit in no- mi- ne do- mi- ni. O- san- na in ex- cel- sis.

Agnus dei
PBN 1112

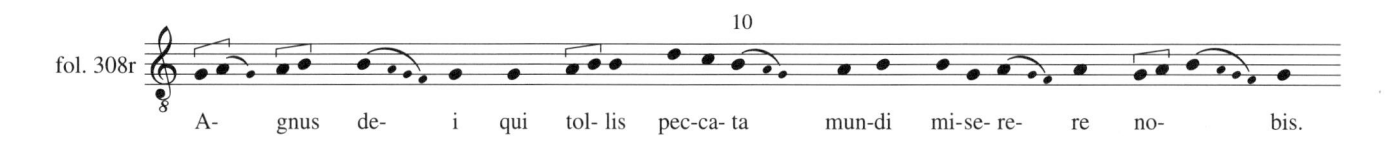

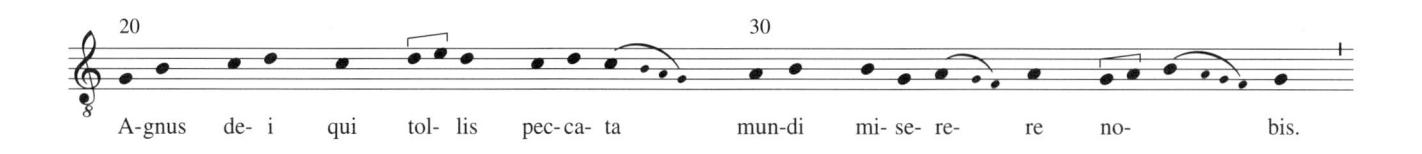

[musical notation, fol. 308r]

A- gnus de- i qui tol- lis pec-ca- ta mun-di mi-se- re- re no- bis.

A-gnus de- i qui tol- lis pec-ca- ta mun-di mi- se- re- re no- bis.

A- gnus de- i qui tol- lis pec-ca- ta mun-di do-na no- bis pa- cem.

Critical Notes

Sanctus: PBN 1112

This chant is taken from the trope *Sanctus Perpetuo numine* of PBN 1112. For the purposes of this edition, I have excerpted the PBN 1112 trope in order to isolate the parent chant. Check marks above the staff indicate where the trope has been omitted. The music of PBN 1112 is written in square notation on a four-line staff. Text underlay is sometimes questionable—the text scribe wrote first and the music scribe wrote above—but can be ascertained by comparison with the following tropes and the W1 tropes.

68: The notes above the staff nearly intersect with the preceding text written immediately above; the top note of the pes D is smudged into an additional virga D, which the scribe probably drew for clarification of pitch.

Sanctus: Reconstructed from W1

This is a composite, reconstructed chant based on the Sanctus of PBN 1112 and variants found or implied in the W1 tropes.

8–11: Each time the third iteration of "Sanctus" appears in the W1 tropes, it is notated with the same music as the first "Sanctus." In contrast, PBN gives a variant for the third "Sanctus" (see the example in the introduction). The W1 version is given here and is used throughout the edition. **17:** This melody is taken from the one notated "sabaoth" found in W1, Fascicle X (*Sanctus Christe yerarchia* [no. 4]). **42 and 71:** This portion of the chant is never given in the W1 tropes. The notes here are reconstructed using the melodic rhyme model of PBN 1112: the notes match the melodic material of W1's third "Sanctus" iteration, just as the corresponding musical cadences of PBN 1112 match the melodic material of its third "Sanctus."

Agnus dei: PBN 1112

55–56: Ligature groups differ slightly from the three W1, Fascicle X, Agnus tropes that have music written out (nos. 10, 12, and 15). W1 groups the first three notes together in ligature, with the second three continuing as currentes. I have used the W1 variation when providing any missing notes for "pacem" in the tropes.